A CUP OF COMFORT®

for Parents *of* Children *with* Special Needs

Stories that celebrate the differences
in our extraordinary kids

Edited by Colleen Sell

Avon, Massachusetts

For Dennis and Junella Sell, with love, admiration, and gratitude, and for Cindy, Gregory, and Christopher, and in loving memory of Donetta and Randall (Buddy) Sell.

Published by
Adams Media, a division of F+W Media, Inc.
57 Littlefield Street, Avon, MA 02322 U.S.A.
www.adamsmedia.com and *www.cupofcomfort.com*

ISBN 10: 1-60550-088-7
ISBN 13: 978-1-60550-088-1
Printed in the United States of America.

J I H G F E D C B A

Library of Congress Cataloging-in-Publication Data
is available from the publisher.

Contents

Acknowledgments

My deepest appreciation goes to my aunt and uncle, Junella and Dennis Sell, for inspiring me with their living example of how to lovingly and effectively parent all children and especially children with special needs.

As always, my thanks go to the top-notch team at Adams Media, particularly Meredith O'Hayre, the *Cup of Comfort*® champion; Paula Munier, the *Cup of Comfort*® creator; the book's copyeditor, Barbara Beaudoin; the book's designer, Ashley Vierra; publicist Jacquinn Williams; and publisher Karen Cooper. Working with such personable and professional people to create such meaningful books is an honor and a joy.

I am most grateful to the authors whose personal stories grace these pages and to you, dear readers, for allowing us to share these very special stories with you.

Introduction

"I think these difficult times have helped me to understand better than before how infinitely rich and beautiful life is in every way and that so many things that one goes around worrying about are of no importance whatsoever."

—*Isak Dinesen*

I am no stranger to adversity. It has been a persistent companion throughout much of my life. But for a long time, when people would comment on my "strength" in dealing with whatever hardship or misfortune had come my way, I'd say, "Feh! It's just life. I can handle it, and eventually, I'll get over it. What I couldn't handle, though, is something happening to one of my kids."

Usually, I would then go on to tell about my Aunt Junella and Uncle Denny, how they have faced what I was certain I could not—again and again. A daughter with Down syndrome and heart defects, their firstborn, who "went to heaven" before her first birthday. A beautiful, brilliant, healthy daughter. A sweet, lovable son with cerebral palsy, an enlarged heart, and severe mental retardation, everyone's "Buddy," who "went home to Jesus" in his late twenties. A handsome, healthy, gregarious son. A stillborn. A handsome, healthy, precocious son felled at age nineteen with a traumatic brain injury that left him a triplegic with minimal use of one hand and a host of cognitive, neurobiological, and health issues. Unfathomable hardship and heartache. And still, they carried on. Still, they found joy in life. Still, no matter how much life has taken from them and out of them, they gave of themselves, tirelessly and graciously, not only to their children but also to others. And still do.

Aunt Nellie and Uncle Denny are like second parents to me, and my family spent a lot of time with their family when I was growing up. I loved going to their house and playing with my cousins, listening to my uncle's jokes and stories, and hearing my aunt's gentle voice and infectious giggle. I loved singing along with Buddy and getting one of his big hugs.

Hugs and laughter were plentiful in my aunt and uncle's home. Although there was plenty of cause for sorrow, tears were few. Patience and prayers were abundant. It was one of the few places where I felt truly accepted, safe, and loved.

It was there that I learned to feel compassion for those less fortunate and to embrace people whose mental and physical abilities are different from the "norm."

My aunt and uncle's life story has given me the insight and the inspiration to be a better parent and a better human being. It has helped me to better handle and provide for my children's special needs. And it has enabled me to better appreciate the things that really matter—the infinite riches and beauty of life.

This book is filled with similarly remarkable stories—most written by parents of children with special needs, with a few by siblings of those with special needs, and by people who were once children with special needs. I trust their personal stories will comfort and inspire you, just as my very special aunt and uncle and their very special children have inspired me.

Enjoy!

—Colleen Sell

A Life Less Perfect

Before my son Nicholas was born, my life was perfect. I ran in an invisible race with neighbors and friends, a race to see who had the greenest lawn, the smartest kids, and the whitest teeth. I was a member of an elite group, devoted to raising elite children. We spent our lives at barbecues and soccer games, tallying our points in our quest to grab that glittering gold ring of perfection.

As we admired our children and our lawns, we never stopped to realize that on our faces we wore rose-colored glasses and in our hearts we felt an emptiness that searched for a deeper meaning to our lives.

On January 18, 2002, like a thin layer of glass, my perfect life came shattering down by the purest sound of six horrifying words: "Your son has Prader-Willi syndrome."

Suddenly, I could not breathe. I sobbed for my child. I sobbed for myself. I sobbed for the perfect life we would never have together. There were no flowers, no cards, no congratulatory notes from family and friends. My son entered the world in silence. No smiles, no laughter, no fanfare. No one welcomed him; everyone was sad. Where in a perfect world would this little child fit? It was as if his very existence threatened to tarnish this utopian world we had created. My tiny son was a giant monster of truth that threatened to expose the meaninglessness of a life built out of playing cards. All who lived in these fragile card houses could not understand how to celebrate the birth of this little child.

My son lay limp upon his hospital bed. A yellow feeding tube was taped harshly to his soft cheek; it traveled up his nose and into his stomach. To his soft skull another plastic tube was taped, pumping antibiotics into his fragile veins. Around his floppy body, a brace made out of thick straps and stiff Velcro held his weakened hips in place. Feeding machines and intravenous poles surrounded him like quiet metal soldiers standing at attention. Everywhere, alarms sounded, a constant reminder that this was hell and we now lived in it. Around me in the neonatal intensive care unit, I saw only despair—parents with children struggling to live.

Like my newly born infant, I was abruptly and cruelly removed from the warmth of my womb-like life. I was thrust headfirst into a cold and terrifying world. This was my new home. I felt sick. Every movement I made felt unnatural and awkward. My mind was numb. My body moved purposelessly. I did not want to look around me, for everywhere I looked, I saw only pain. I felt like a soldier on a battlefield, frozen by the ghastly sight of the slain, bloody carcasses at his feet. Yet, like a soldier in a war he did not create, I too could not escape my fate.

The rose-colored glasses I once blindly wore were smashed into smithereens. My eyes, unaccustomed to this new light, could not stop crying. In his sad and traumatic entrance into this world, my imperfect son had given me an unwelcome gift—the gift of sight, the ability to see the world not as I wanted it but as it truly was. I saw the pain and sadness, the frailty of life.

When he finally came home from the hospital, I had to hold my infant carefully or his head would flop quickly forward. When it did, he could not breathe. I felt helpless. I questioned God. What had I done to my son? I felt guilty. When I took him out into the world, people would stare and ask why he had a tube in his nose. I felt embarrassed. When I handed my fragile child to the doctor at the children's hospital for eye surgery, I felt scared. So many endless days brought so many endless, hurtful, hard emotions. I felt so very tired.

When my tired body and exhausted soul seemed like it could bear no more, my floppy little child began to get stronger. As he did, I began to feel a lost emotion, happiness.

After almost a year, Nicholas held up his head. That tiny infant who'd struggled to breathe was now able to see the world. I felt joy. When his g-tube was removed and the words "failure to thrive" were removed from his chart, I released the breath I had held since his birth. When he pushed away his metal walker and took steps for the first time, I wept.

Slowly, I began to realize that these tortuous feelings and hardships were important. These awful extremes of emotion gave my life new meaning. I understood myself better. I understood others a lot better. Although these emotions left me feeling fragile and vulnerable, I couldn't help but wonder if that was God's intention.

As I became accustomed to my new sight, I saw we were surrounded here on Earth by many disguised angels—intelligent, kind, compassionate human beings devoted to curing and healing the sick. Why hadn't I seen them before? Why hadn't I appreciated them? Once again, this imperfect child had opened my eyes. I could now see these special souls who travel among us, these selfless, gifted, healing guardians who would now be a part of our lives forever. Wrapped in their wings, this horrifying new life of ours seemed a little less scary.

Other earthly angels also became visible to me for the first time: parents of other children with Prader-Willi syndrome whose paths were as treacherous as ours. Via an Internet chat group, we special few shared our advice, our tears, and our love. A unique brotherhood was forged, for we could truly understand each other. I listened to the words of these parents I had never met. I listened to these strangers with quiet hearts, and somehow my hardened spirit became a little lighter. Why? I do not know, because I was still sad. But somehow, by releasing my tears and listening to others, I began to accept and understand this challenging life.

I began to accept that my son is not like others in this world. I began to accept that this is not a curse, but a blessing. To me, Nicholas is unusually happy, loving, and kind. I am amazed by his keen perception of human beings and his unique ability to engage even the grumpiest of personalities. He lives to dance and laugh and love. He has a warm heart and a gentle spirit, and although he is my child, he has also been my teacher.

Each of us is blessed with special gifts, and although my son's gifts are hidden, buried beneath a weakened body, his gifts are no less special. I do not have a son who can run very fast. I have a son with the precious gifts of empathy and human compassion.

I now realize that my life with Nicholas will not be like the lives of so many others. It will not be an ordinary life. It will be, it is, an extraordinary life—a life filled with high highs and low lows. I would not trade one day of feeling that terrible pain, because I know now the terrible happiness that is waiting on the other side for me. What I have learned is to appreciate both. For it is these feelings, this blending of the good and the bad, that somehow bring me closer to understanding my purpose here on Earth. This awareness, this blending of heart and spirit, has helped me to embrace my son and to enjoy this journey we are sharing together.

It is a sad, sweet, beautiful trip. It is a life less perfect. It is a life more meaningful.

—Lisa Peters

This story first appeared in the National Newsletter of the Prader-Willi Syndrome Association *(USA), May/June 2007.*

Reach and Pull

Ruth's eyes twinkled like the lights reflecting off the water of the pool. She held the orange safety cone up to her mouth, using it as a make-shift megaphone. "And now, ladies and gentlemen, it's time to watch the amazing Nick as he attempts to swim to the other side of the pool. Come on, Nick, let's see you reach and pull, reach and pull. That's the way! Use those arms to swim across the water."

I inhaled sharply as my son, wearing his favorite red goggles, gasped a big breath and bobbed across the surface. Maybe I took a breath every time his mouth tilted sideways for air and his arm came up and over. Maybe my feet kicked just a little bit underneath the chair where I sat and watched. I was on the edge of my seat, and it felt more like watching an Olympic event than a beginning swimming class.

It had taken a long time for my son to reach this level of skill and confidence. Nick has autism, and just about every activity outside our home posed huge challenges for both him and me. There was the indoor kinder-gym, where we lasted about three visits, until one day my son took all the riding cars and carefully lined them up, refusing to let anyone touch his creation, and screamed bloody murder when they tried. That (understandably) didn't go over very well with the other parents or kids.

He had had a very rough time at two or three preschools. There was the time he hurled birdseed all over the room and into everyone's hair. Yes, it could have landed in an eye; thank goodness, it didn't. Then there were the dreaded circle times, where all the children (except him) sat down compliantly and sang songs and listened to stories. It was nearly impossible for Nick to participate in circle time. He usually sat somewhere on the other side of the room, constructing walls of giant, red cardboard blocks and then sending them crashing down.

The last preschool attempt, even though he was only enrolled part-time, ended in disaster. He had frequent tantrums, and his behavior was unpredictable. The day he wandered off into the parking lot during class time was when I finally pulled him out for good. I just wanted to keep him home and keep him safe.

Even at the pool, I had to accompany him as his one-on-one assistant into the pool for a long while. It was my job to keep him focused and to literally hold him in one spot so he could listen to and follow the teacher's instructions. At times, he just wouldn't listen and had to take time-outs, sitting on the edge of the pool. There were times when I wondered if it was worth the hassle.

But we persisted. For more than a year, every Tuesday and Thursday I rounded up Nick and his brother Ben, their suits and towels, and headed to the pool. I used to pass the mothers who sat in the lobby, watching their children through a big glass window participate in the group class. They would casually talk with each other or read magazines. It was like they actually got a—GASP—break! Yes, I admit it, at times I was jealous.

Still, I was so grateful that the Easter Seal Pool offered semi-private lessons and that we had managed to snag spots for my two sons. It was worth the hassle of getting us there on time and suiting up in the ladies' dressing room to play in the water for thirty minutes.

Nick and Ben were water babies from the beginning. They loved choosing from the multicolored goggles that their teacher, Ruth, had to offer, and they often haggled over who got the red ones. They floated on foam mats, learned breathing techniques, and played with rubber duckies. Ruth was one of the first teachers who could really get through to Nick. She never seemed to mind when he yelled, got upset, or wouldn't try. She was gentle, cheerful, and persistent. I never once saw her with dry hair.

Ruth came up with fun, creative ways to teach. One of the boys' favorites was learning the elementary backstroke, which she playfully called "chicken, airplane, soldier." First position, you look like a chicken with your arms pulled up like wings; second position, arms go out like an airplane; third position, they end at your sides like a soldier.

Ben, seventeen months younger than Nick, learned everything faster. He had no fear of diving for colored beads or jumping into the deep water. After about a year of lessons, he could easily swim from one end of the pool to the other and was ready to move on to new activities. Nick, on the other hand, could do a sort of modified dog-paddle and was terrified of leaving the shallow end of the pool.

After eighteen months, Ben went to preschool, and I had to switch Nick to private lessons. They were more expensive, but, again, well worth it. I finally got to sit in the lobby and read back issues of *Ladies' Home Journal* and occasionally talk with other moms. It was a liberating thirty minutes.

Ruth grew very fond of Nick, too, especially when she had him all to herself. She would often end the lesson a little early and take Nick into the hot tub, where she'd practice Watsu, an aquatic therapy, with him. She held him ever so gently as he floated on his back, very much like a babe in the womb. Nick grew quiet and still during these precious moments. He momentarily relaxed and felt safe with another, something so rare in his sensory-overloaded life.

Now, day after day of practice and routine had glided us all to this moment. There was Ruth with her orange cone megaphone, I behind the glass wall, and Nick on his own in the middle of the pool. Steadily, he swam across the water. To me, it seemed as wide as the Atlantic Ocean. When he made it across, his little hand went out and grasped the edge of the pool.

For a moment he looked over at me, and I waved frantically. I thought I caught a trace of a smile before he lunged back into the water, surprising us all with a final crossing. Ruth put the cone down and screamed and clapped for him to bring it on home. As I watched my son reach and pull, reach and pull, my heart beat with every stroke he made. My little soldier swam to victory, over the deep end and past the shallows, into the arms of Ruth.

—Elizabeth King Gerlach

Thump, Thump, Kerthump

Thump, thump, kerthump. Thump, thump, kerthump.

There is a strange sound emanating from the hallway. It's like a series of sounds, of thuds, punctuated by an odd, louder noise. The hallway is narrow, so there isn't much room for a five-year-old to create too much havoc. I close my eyes, and as I try to visualize the corresponding sequence of events, the rhythm is interrupted by a much louder sound—*kersplat!*—and the house shakes. I realize a child has fallen against the wall. I listen intently, but no one is crying. After a brief pause, the sounds continue.

Thump, thump, kerthump. Thump, thump, kerthump. Thump, thump, kersplat! Once more, the house shakes. He has hit the wall again.

I want to give him space, but my curiosity is getting the better of me. What are these noises? His twin brother is outside with his dad, so it can't be some crazy new game of slam-each-other-against-the-wall.

"I'm okay, Mom," he calls out, as if to reassure both of us, but his voice is thin and quivers slightly.

The sounds continue.

Thump, thump, kerthump. Thump, thump, kerthump. I tiptoe to the hallway and stealthily peer around the corner. As soon as I see him, I feel the hot sting of my tears and quickly put my hand over my mouth. I know what he is doing.

He is hopping on his left foot, his better leg. He is very unsteady, teetering as if he is riding an invisible unicycle, with his arms spread like wings. I see that they are serving double-duty, not only helping him to balance but also to right himself by pushing against the wall if he leans too much to one side or the other. I marvel at his ingenuity—our hallway is the perfect place for a five-year-old to practice hopscotch.

One foot, one foot, both feet. *Thump, thump, kerthump.*

But then he falls—*kersplat!*—his left leg and both his arms failing him. In an instant, he is up and the cycle starts again.

He has been at it for a while, and he will keep plugging away until he is satisfied. That is his style. My son, Victor, does not know that two words, *cerebral palsy*, hang around his neck like off-set ballast. His arms and legs are stiff, and his balance is precarious, at best. He falls a lot; he has to sit to get dressed; and he is much slower than other kids on the playground. You can see in his face that every movement is a carefully constructed orchestration.

Born at twenty-six weeks gestation, almost four months early, he and his twin have already endured more than a lifetime of hardship. But it was Victor who came home from the intensive care unit with a twisted right side. Ever since, he has struggled to do so many things that we "able-bodied" people take for granted.

However, what really separates Victor from almost everyone else is his sheer determination. He doesn't understand "can't," only "try harder." And so he will practice and practice and practice, long after I can feign interest in continuing. His therapists shake their heads and smile in disbelief at his progress, but the credit lies with Victor. In the beginning, I helped out a lot more, but now he only allows me to show him once and then he will take it from there, thank you very much.

If we are running late, I can try to speed up the process, but it will be to no avail. "I want to do it," he'll say with surprising force for such a small body as he snatches his sneakers from my hand. God forbid if I manage to distract him long enough to slip on his socks; time will have to stand still while he takes them off and puts them on again—by himself. And so we are often late. There are some things that you just have to accept.

I often wonder if Victor knows he is different, although, thanks to his absolute persistence, what physically separates him from his peers is getting increasingly harder for the untrained eye to see. Is his tenacity a reflection of his stubborn personality (no idea where that came from) or does it derive from his own observation of his limitations? Regardless, when Victor decides that he will do something, he simply does not give up until he has mastered the task or at least achieved a close semblance.

And today he wants to play hopscotch. He saw some older girls playing at the schoolyard, and he loves older girls, so he will be in the hallway for as long as it takes. Last year he spent weeks launching himself from our front steps so he could learn to land on both feet like the other kids. He is now the undisputed frog king.

Thump. Thump. Kerthump. Thump, thump, kerthump. I feel it in my chest as if my heartbeat depends on each tentative hop.

To stand by and do nothing while your child falls and then falls again is torture, but I cannot look away. I am his mother, and it is my job to bear witness. I am simultaneously transfixed, awestruck, and filled with pride by both his effort and his success.

The sound of his voice whisks me back from my short reverie and the hallway slides into focus. He doesn't stop as he speaks; there is no time for that.

"Mom, look." *Thump.* "I can." *Thump.* "Hopscotch!" *Kerthump.*

I smile and fight back the tears. "Great job," I manage to squeak before hurrying back to the kitchen, where I dissolve on the spot. His spirit and willpower never cease to amaze me. And I understand that I am a better person for knowing him.

The next day, we go to the schoolyard, and for an hour that could have lasted all day, Victor hopped up and down the playground on his left foot, with both of us wearing smiles of sheer joy and my heart bursting at the seams.

Thump, thump, kerthump. Thump, thump, kerthump. A week later, the noises start again. I sneak over to the hallway. He is now working on his right leg.

Victor may have cerebral palsy, but cerebral palsy does not have Victor.

—Jennifer Gunter

Expletives Deleted

There was a time when my husband and I believed that raising a hearing-impaired child was the most complicated and worrisome burden ever required of a parent. Eventually, we would come to understand that all children (including our one deaf child and our two "normal" children) come equipped with idiosyncrasies that make them distinct and similarities that blur the distinctions, no matter how blatant they originally seem.

When we learned our newborn daughter Rachel was profoundly deaf, our list of worries was long. Primary was the concern that she would never learn to talk. My husband and I would have been reassured, I suppose, if we could have foreseen the future and the time when we would actually request of Rachel, "Would you please, for heaven's sake, be quiet, for just five minutes?"

As worried as we were about our daughter's chances of ever speaking coherently, we could certainly never have predicted a time when we would want to censor her communication.

From the time Rachel was diagnosed as profoundly deaf and then fitted with hearing aids on her first birthday, my husband and I were ever diligent about bombarding her with sounds. "Did you hear that?" we'd ask her when a dog barked or a train whistled or a horn blared. That she didn't hear sounds in the environment, much less speech, most of the time didn't stop us from trying.

Our kitchen table became a makeshift learning center filled with toys, plastic animals, and noise makers.

"The cow says, 'Mooooooo,'" we'd intone. "The airplane goes, 'Vroooooom.'" "Baaaby, baaaby, baaaby. See the baby? Hear it cry? Waaaaaaaaahhhhhh!"

Even though the results were sometimes modest, all through her toddler years we spoon-fed Rachel the sounds and the vocabulary that our other two children picked up without assistance. Teaching Rachel became a family affair, and her siblings joined in as we repeated, enunciated, elaborated, and talked and talked and talked some more to try to fill that walking database with language. By the time Rachel's younger brother was three years old, he had been exposed to a lifetime of speech therapy, causing his preschool teacher to remark that she had never heard a child enunciate his words so clearly.

Of course, we studiously avoided inputting "bad" words. Our other two children were quick to catch the slightest unintentional slip of the tongue. But Rachel, because she had to read our lips to supplement her limited hearing, missed out on this part of her socialization. In a naïve way, we assumed that she would reach adulthood without exposure to profanity.

Occasionally, when sounds and words began to stick, Rachel's pronunciations were unique, to say the least. For instance, she referred to the lower female anatomy as her "vashanka." We chose not to correct her, as we were afraid that the clearly pronounced word would be the one that everyone would understand when she shouted it out in a public place.

"I ate you," she learned to say later, meaning she hated me or another family member, but losing the value of the softly spoken *h*. At times, Rachel was clearly frustrated by her lack of vocabulary, particularly when it came to battling with her siblings. She once consulted the dictionary and, based on the ugliest animal she could lay eyes upon, called her brother a water buffalo, an insult that did not exactly have the impact she had hoped for.

Still, for the most part, expletives were deleted from her vocabulary.

Upon receiving a cochlear implant at the age of eleven, Rachel began playing catch-up. For the first time ever, she actually could hear the dog bark and the baby cry and the coyote howl. She could hear the wind in the trees and the frogs on the pond as well as all manner of irritating daily noises that the rest of us tuned out on a regular basis. Our first trip to the beach after her cochlear implant, Rachel heard the ocean for the first time ever, an emotional event for the whole family.

Intensive speech therapy helped her to more clearly pronounce the words she was finally beginning to hear. After months of practice, she could actually eavesdrop on a conversation without the use of sign language or lip reading. New doors were opening for our daughter, some of which we had never anticipated.

One day I picked Rachel up from middle school. My daughter had barely gotten in the car when she began questioning me excitedly about a new word she had learned from her best friend.

"I'm not calling you this," she kept reassuring me before she finally spelled it out, both aloud and on her fingers: "B-i-t-c-h."

Rachel wasn't very impressed with the female dog definition of the word and rushed me along until I told her it could also refer to a very mean woman. Apparently, I hit closer to home with this description. Rachel went on to say that there was a b-i-t-c-h in her physical education class. That's what she'd overheard, anyway. Then she wanted to know how to pronounce this new word, and I relented, giving her the proper sounds to speak it correctly. After all, I reasoned, she had a right to know how to pronounce such a word so that she wouldn't confuse some floozy who might wonder why she was being called a beach.

Finally, with a little bit of embarrassment, Rachel thanked me for my help and reiterated that she just hadn't known that word. Then, by way of comparison, she added, "I don't know what mango means either."

Trying to help her appreciate the humor of the situation, I asked, "Did your friend call anyone a mango?"

"No," she said in all seriousness, "just a bitch."

A few weeks later, Rachel became angry when I refused to help her with her homework.

"Mean bitch," I heard her mutter under her breath.

"What did you call me?" I repeated the question several more times before Rachel sheepishly admitted the insult.

I sent her to her room while deciding on the proper punishment to administer, just as I would with any of my kids. But I have to admit to a different feeling when the shock wore off. I'd call it a tiny spark of pride: Pride that my imperfect, struggling child responded to her mother in such a normal, though admittedly inappropriate, adolescent way. Pride that she knew enough not to call me a mango when the chips were down. And pride that her pronunciation was perfect.

—Ellen Ward

This story first appeared in Hearing Health, *Winter 2001.*

Finding Rest, Off-Center

"Don't be so high up on your pillow." I couldn't resist correcting. "Your new bed has plenty of leg room."

Buddy nodded and snuggled his five-foot, ten-inches deeper into the bed sheets. Then he sat up to share our nightly bless and hug.

It didn't matter that my son was fifteen, going on sixteen. It didn't matter that he couldn't count to ten, would never drive a car, go to college, or ever empty the nest. Evenings, I needed his arms flopped around my back, his head on my right shoulder. And Buddy needed Mom's fingers to scratch his black hair and her lips to speak a blessing over him.

He needed his sleep and his daytime life to be blessed with rest for his nerves, affected by seizures. My nerves frayed through his emergencies. Over time

I learned to rely on a treasured way to find peace in the tangle of medical and mommy anxieties.

But I almost lost my peace that bed-making day.

"No! I want it . . . the same place, Mom," Buddy begged. His tanned hands clutched the corner of his new mattress.

"Look," I explained, "it's easier to make the bed away from the wall."

"I want it the same place, the same place," he repeated as always.

My Filipina emotions flared. "Buddy, I want your bed centered! It's easier for me to make your bed away from the wall."

While we dittoed back and forth positions, my all-American hubby, Bud's dad, stepped in for the compromise. He moved the queen-sized bed off center, scrunched it against Bud's nightstand, which was scrunched against the inner corner of the bedroom at our new house.

Like painters attacking fresh canvas, we three made that off-centered bed. Around his pillow-top mattress we wrapped indigo sheets of Egyptian cotton. Over those sheets we layered a navy-blue blanket. Over that blanket we smoothed a navy-blue, baffle box comforter filled with goose down. Periwinkle willow leaves scattered over the new bed comforter, like sailboats on a tranquil sea. Buddy placed two new pillows in Egyptian cotton cases, then stuffed two extra pillows into matching shams.

Dad and Buddy left the bedroom. Through the back window I viewed our old house, to the west on an opposite Pennsylvanian hillside. There, our son's restless nights had begun a dozen years before in a crib. After he grew into a wiggly toddler, we moved him over to a single mate's bed, set at a right angle to the upper captain's bunk bed of our eldest son.

Almost nightly, our youngest woke on that low bed, screaming wildly in tears. Sometimes we blamed thunder storms. But my husband and I spent many clear nights stretched out on the floor beside the little bed.

In that old house, I thought Buddy had little room to settle into sleep, his bed flat against a cold wall with no insulation. I tried to ease his single mattress out an inch or two from that wall whenever I could. But he forced the mattress flush to the wall, especially after one fateful December night.

At three o'clock that morning I bolted up as hard knocks broke the odd silence.

"Mom, Dad!" my eldest yelled through the door. "I think Bud's having a seizure!"

We found our then nine-year-old wedged between his bed and the wall. My heart clenched as I saw his head banging into the wall. My daughter Jessica and

I cried out to God. My husband and son Michael rushed to carefully extract sweet Buddy.

From age three on, Buddy took medication for infrequent, strong seizures. These severe seizures made him eligible for an FDA trial on Diastat, a Valium delivery system. Now, I called the study's nurse for permission to administer, as my husband prepped the syringe.

"Mom, ouch! Daddy!" Buddy moaned later, on a hospital gurney headed to a lab.

Exams showed no concussion and no skull fractures. But I knew X-rays wouldn't reveal the true damage.

Previous seizures had battered his speech and motor developments. Because viruses triggered these seizures, we home-schooled our son. Hours and hours, year after year, in concert with specialists, we pursued speech, occupational, and physical therapies along with intense, repetitive instruction. Before that December episode, we'd just begun to teach him—wonder of wonders—second grade, double-digit math.

To our dismay, Buddy's December seizures were a combo tsunami-cyclone. They swirled away verbal and academic gains. How I wished those seizures had instead seized his memory of the terrors between the wall and the bed.

Driving him home from the hospital days later, I heard an ambulance siren in the distance. I also heard my boy start to babble. Or so I thought.

"What, honey?" I asked.

"Mumble, mumble . . . Gee-sus, be with . . . mumble, mumble."

Stopped at the intersection, I peered at his reflection in the rear-view mirror. He was praying for the patient in the ambulance! Tears dripped past my glasses.

Often, I find myself asking God, "Would you heal (someone's name)?"

Buddy often prays a declaration: "You can heal him. You can heal her." My boy rests in a child's assured faith, while I, in my adult faith, can't seem to rest or relax. Though we had taught him to pray, his words taught me the one I could trust in each day.

Over the next eighteen months, the family worked hard to restore Buddy's academic memories. Intelligence tests indicated our boy could receive information, but neural disconnects kept him from easily telling us or writing down what he understood. Though he grew to be a caring, chatty, social butterfly, his academic lessons fell into mental minefields that blew up and mangled his math facts and his ability to express what he had learned whenever he had another seizure.

Seizure events seemed to crowd our tiny, dark, first home. We moved to a larger place with an open floor plan. Upstairs were separate bedrooms for the three kids. Bud's new bedroom had a messy old bed, which clung to a new wall. I continued the evening hugs and blesses. Mornings, I prepped him for public school entry.

At the Sunrise School for Exceptional Children, fifteen-year-old Buddy had tested at the second-grade math level. Three years before, his doctor weaned him off all daily anti-seizure medication.

Suddenly, it seemed, my son stood nine inches over me. He'd outgrown his clothes. He'd outgrown his shoes. His body no longer fit the leftover link to that terrifying night. It was time to buy a bigger bed.

"Just an excuse to go shopping, go shopping," Buddy quickly rattled to tease me about my fun habit. I had to go and shop, I told him. He needed a bigger mattress for the periwinkle bedding just arrived from Home Shopping Network.

The morning after his first night in the queen-sized bed, Buddy's big feet thumped downstairs to the kitchen.

"Mom, it's hard to get out, hard to get out." His dark eyes twinkled, as a sloppy grin spread across his face.

"So you like the new bed," I deduced.

"Mom, I made my bed. I made my bed."

I walked upstairs. Over the bed was stretched a smoothed comforter, a bit off kilter, and two sham pillows, a bit off kilter. Still, the periwinkle leaves scattered over the comforter like sailboats on a calm sea.

For six consecutive years, Buddy had no episodes. But after two ambulance trips to the emergency room, he went back on his anti-seizure medication. Emotionally tipped off-center, I wept and wept. Then I remembered how my very special son releases his worries. Buddy still can't count to ten, but he continues to bow his head and say, "You can heal." So now, when life tilts off center and beyond my control, I follow his lead . . . and I rest.

As for that off-centered bed, on most days it's messy, no longer from seizures but from frenzied, early morning rises. Weekends, we try to return it to a "sailor's delight." Regardless, every night at bedtime—even though Bud turned twenty and sports a mustache—I still bless and hug him while he holds his blue, fuzzy Jungle Book bear. And through the night, the family sleeps to the lullaby of Bud's crunchy snores.

—Cynthia Agricola Hinkle

Peanut Butter Toast

So my son set the house on fire. Good story, this. People love it at parties. Here's how it goes.

Nikolai, who is five years old, was born with Williams syndrome. It's a rare genetic defect, a deletion of the elastin gene on the seventh chromosome. Sound like gibberish to you? It did to me, too. Let's break it down into real-person speak.

Niko doesn't have enough stretchy stuff in his body to grow properly. He has problems with his heart and his lungs. His body is very stiff. He has some mental retardation and some learning disabilities. He doesn't speak yet, but he will, and then, whoa boy! Williams kids tend to parrot, to repeat everything that they hear regardless of whether it's appropriate to say such things. If they hear it, they say it, and Niko's mama has a big mouth. One day, perhaps soon, five and counting years of being a loudmouth mama and having a nonverbal child are going to catch up with me. I'm planning on moving about then. I say this with a smile, but I'm already packing my belongings.

As a baby, Niko threw up everything he ate, and eventually went on medication for severe gastroesophageal reflux disease (GERD). As an end result, he has an aversion to most foods. Anything cold or creamy, like yogurt or oatmeal? No way. Niko is a dry/crunchy kind of kid and has one true love: peanut butter toast.

Hooray for peanut butter! Full of protein for building muscle on my skinny boy, and it's easy to manage. Attractive, too. Most days, my pants are adorned with a peanut-butter handprint, compliments of my sweet child.

Anyway, back to the fire.

One day, as usual, Niko wants toast. He loves toast, can't get enough of peanut butter toast. He can't ask me with words, so he usually brandishes a butter knife at me, my cue that he's asking for his PBT. Suddenly, though, he decides he wants to be independent, and that's when everything goes awry.

Dad is at work, and Mama is busy taking care of Baby Sister, a sweet little thing with triumphant pigtails. This is Niko's time to shine.

He goes to the toaster, pushes it down. That's what Mama does when she's making toast. It pops up, but no toast. Niko pushes it down again; waits. It pops up, but no toast. Now, I have no idea how long he repeats this process, toasting the phantom bread that never made it into the toaster, but suddenly he's at my side making "uh uh!" sounds in a way that tells me something is wrong. My boy doesn't speak, but that doesn't mean he doesn't communicate. He has sounds for happy, sounds for sad. His eyes are starry and incredibly expressive. And right now, they're broadcasting fear.

"Show me," I say.

Grabbing my hand, he leads me from his sister's room. To the kitchen. Where the toaster is on fire. The flames start licking their way up the cupboards.

This is what my mind does: it shuts down. Fire. And then it starts to whirr. Fire!

We don't have an extinguisher. I have two little kids, neither of which have the presence of mind to avoid the flames. I take it all in. How fast it's moving, so horrifically fast. How fragile my children are. How I never would have known about it had Niko not told me.

I grab hot pads, paw at the toaster. I don't have much of a choice. I go to throw the toaster in the sink, but the flames are too high. I rush through the kitchen, open the sliding glass door with my elbow, and toss the toaster outside on the patio. I hold the kids on my lap, and we watch the toaster until it burns out. It's a blackened, charred thing, smelling of electrical wire and smoke. It's awful.

Niko brings me a butter knife. He wants peanut butter toast.

I can't get the smell out of the house for days. We sleep with the windows open, the fans blowing. I'm cleaning soot off of the cupboards and walls. I'm seeing the black spots where the fire burned underneath the cupboard. I notice that I'm crying off and on during those days.

Here's the thing: Having a child with special needs is hard. Sure, you know that, you think I'm stating the obvious. But it is. It's amazing and wonderful and teaches you things that you would never in a million years learn otherwise. But it's horrendously, painfully hard, and every now and then something comes along to remind you of just how tough it can really be.

I live in panic mode. That's just the way that it is. I never know if today is going to be the day that Niko's body simply gives up. I never know if today is going to be the day that something snaps or breaks, and he won't be able to tell me about it. I don't know if he's crying because he's upset or because his stomach hurts or because his heart has exhausted itself beyond its own endurance. I have a son who can't tell me if his teacher hurts him at school, who can't tell me about the things that he saw. He can't get himself dressed and can't make his own decisions. I wonder if he'll ever fall in love or travel, or even if he'll want to do these things. Will he live at home forever? Will he be happy if he does? Will I know the difference?

I have a five-year-old who can't make his own toast. He nearly burns the house down when he tries.

Then one day I get a grip on myself and move on. Though I think it's okay to be sad sometimes, grieving for the life that I wanted for my child, I know I need to pull up my garters and go. Special needs children aren't about grief; they're about hope. I know he's happy. He has his backyard and his little sister and his Cookie Monster. We wrap him in his blanket and read to him every night. He jumps on the trampoline and gives me kisses. This is definitely a house of kisses.

Every day Niko learns something new, and so do I. I am learning patience. And responsibility. I'm learning that some expectations are unrealistic and to let them go. This doesn't apply only to my son, but to everybody in my life. I'm learning how to really appreciate others without expecting them to be anything different than what they are. Niko's making me a better person. I'm more compassionate. Smarter. I don't make the same mistakes twice.

Now, I unplug the toaster.

—*Mercedes M. Yardley*

A Ferry Tale

On the world's most gloriously sunny day, thirteen-year-old Sophie, her twelve-year-old brother Moe, and I decide it would be a grand idea to set off on an adventure on land and sea. So we board a ferry to sail across the waves to the city of San Francisco.

Once on deck, a whirlwind from the bay blows our hair and clothes, but the sun keeps us cozy and warm. Moe and Sofe run up and down the stairs of the ferry, finally settling outside on the swaying deck. As they always do, strangers try not to stare at the differences in my daughter's features: her shorter stature, her awkward gait, her eyes the shape of almonds—the roadmap of her disability, Down syndrome. Oblivious to any awkwardness, Sophie peers through the red plastic binoculars she's brought along, searching for monster killer whales she is sure she will encounter. On one side of us is the bright orange monolith of the Golden Gate Bridge, on the other we can practically touch Alcatraz.

Braving the fifteen-minute trip like victorious pirates, we disembark at the bustling and touristy Pier 39. After rushing to check out the barking, smelly sea lions, we meander through the stores and food stands. The kids ogle the mini-donut shop, but I persuade them to consider some fish and chips first. Moe chooses where we sit, a red painted picnic table near the stream of tourists. As usual, Sophie gets a splotch of ketchup on her face and doesn't wipe it off. She doesn't seem to notice it at all.

Sophie doesn't have a great sense of her own face and the ketchup-ness thereupon. I'm not sure this lack of vanity is 100 percent a bad quality. I've been told that there is something about the mental and physical disability that my daughter was born with that leaves her unconcerned about this sort of thing. I've been told lots of things about my daughter over the years. But a mother hears things differently than someone else might hear them. I think Sophie's face is exquisite and that ketchup only adds enchantment to a masterpiece. But I know that not everyone thinks that. And I travel a fine line between unconditional love and stoicism when I insist in that moment that she use a napkin.

I help her moisten the paper towel that came with her fish and chips, and we wipe away some of the offending artistry. But my daughter insists upon carrying her leftover ketchup-smeared fries, eating and walking, redoing her impromptu makeup as we make our way along the pier. A veteran, I carry an extra paper towel with me for just such an occurrence.

Little brother Moe is too shy to try the bungee-jumping trampoline attraction at the end of Pier 39, but Sophie begs. "Mom! I want to do that! That looks like fun!" It is one of those heart-sinking moments when I know she can't do it, that her disability does not allow for the physical or mental coordination to actually jump, flip upside down, and land. It is the flipping upside down that is the cool part, the part that I know she cannot accomplish. There is a big crowd watching each kid trying to make the big flip. And, of course, as we stand and watch for a while, each kid, no matter how young, finally flips like a natural circus acrobat. I sigh and feel the familiar inner tug of nervous concern. It is the millionth time I have sighed for my daughter's challenges. Then, I think, *Well, even if she isn't able to flip, at least Sophie will be able to jump on the trampoline. I should buck up and just let her try.*

Moe and I wait, anxious and watchful, as the attendant straps her into the safety harness.

Moe whispers to me, "Mom, what if she shouts, 'Get me down! Get me down!'?"

"I think it will be okay, Moe," I reassure him, as if I knew.

Moe stands close to me, the two of us separate from the other world of regular parents, regular families. Moe has only one sister, and it is Sofe. To him, this is how sisters are. He loves her in that way that we grownups probably forget we ever loved our siblings, as if she were his other heart.

The attendant helps Sophie jump by giving her a little push. Sofe tries valiantly to twirl upside down but seems clumsy, unable to do it. I keep a smile glued to my face. My stomach tightens. The noisy crowd watches. She is all alone up there. The attendant helps her again. She is jumping, and Moe and I are shouting encouragement.

No go.

Then all of a sudden she twirls and flips around just right! Then again! And a third time! Moe is clapping, and I am whooping like a maniac mom at a Little League game.

Sofe is finally lowered onto the mat, flushed with happiness and success. As she scrambles down the exit ramp, I give her a giant high-five. Moe hugs her, beaming.

The three of us celebrate with an ice cream cone for Sophie and a milkshake for Moe at the Cannery. Moe proclaims his the smoothest, creamiest milkshake he's ever had. Sophie adds vanilla ice cream to the collage on her cheeks. To top off the perfect moment, an outside stage musician puts his shiny saxophone to his lips and plays a sweet and soaring rendition of "I Left My Heart in San Francisco."

As we float back home with the crowds on the lumbering ferry, I suddenly have a realization as to why people glance surreptitiously at us when Sophie is close by. It must be because they are envious—thinking, *What perfect, beautiful, and bright children that mother has.*

—Jolie Kanat

Party Plans

"Ronald's having a bowling party this Saturday," he said, avoiding my eyes the way he does when he's worried. "They were passing out invitations at the bowling league."

As I read the card, our seven-year-old son George darted past me and ran through the kitchen. He vaulted back in and dashed out again, his blond curls bouncing as he rounded the corner. George has bipolar disorder. Misdiagnosed as having attention deficit hyperactivity disorder more than a year earlier, he was prescribed Ritalin, and the stimulant exacerbated his mania. The major tranquilizers we gave him afterward had yet to extinguish his perpetual motion.

Before his bipolar diagnosis at age six, George's behaviors—boa-like hugs that started out exuberant and ended in a squeeze so tight the recipient couldn't inhale; scattering pens and cups off of countertops as he ran by; accidentally breaking fish tanks; toppling planters; and marring walls with paint, crayons, and sidewalk chalk—caused even our closest friends to stop inviting him to their parties. Other children spent their weekends piling into vans and traveling to backyards, amusement parks, and zoos for play dates and to celebrate birthdays. Not George. Now, in my hand, I held George's first party invitation in two years. Could I make this work?

I still kept the picture of Dan and George sitting at the preschool table, arms draped around each other's shoulders. Dan was George's best friend when they were three. By the time George had turned four, the differences between him and other children had grown more evident. Seeking stimulation, George climbed on tables during naptime, chewed on dice and game pieces, and caused disruptions whenever he tried to enter into games with other children. I took him to a park to teach him how to play catch; he ran around and kicked trees instead. Soon, George had no friends.

George's disorder had isolated him and our family. If I made George's participation in this party a success, might that lead to more invitations—and to friendships?

I found him standing in the middle of the small hallway between my bedroom and the family room.

Chin up, arms at his sides, feet together and firmly planted in place, George stiffened his body into attention and tilted sideways, using his weight and gravity to propel himself toward the wall. At the last moment, he reached out his stiffened arm and prevented himself from falling. He pushed off toward the opposite wall and swayed like a metronome, back and forth, from one wall to the other.

"George." I squatted at his level to catch his gaze. "What does Ronald want for his birthday?" I asked.

"I don't know." George wore his charging T-Rex tee-shirt. He loved creatures with big teeth, especially carnivorous dinosaurs and great white sharks.

"Ronald's invited you to his birthday party."

George shrugged.

"Will you ask Ronald what he wants for a present?"

"Sure." He smiled with his sparkling green eyes, and then the glint dulled. I recognized that look—George absorbed by his internal distraction. He launched himself toward the wall again. I felt invisible.

When we received the party invitation, it had been only thirteen months since he had received the bipolar diagnosis and started his new medications. Calming a manic exacerbation caused by stimulant treatment takes two years. Every Saturday, I sorted George's medications—Lithium, Tegretol, Seroquel, and Abilify—into a pillbox divided into seven days with three doses per day. Jumping on and off the kitchen table, racing his razor scooter in tight directionless circles, and running out the front door into the street heedless of oncoming traffic were some of the impulsive behaviors that George's doctors said the medication could help stop and that George would learn to mitigate as he matured.

It took us until he was seven to find a supportive school setting and the correct medications to give him a new chance with other kids. Ronald was in George's class. After a few play dates together, George joined Ronald for Wacky Wednesdays, the junior bowling league for elementary students. My husband chuckled when he told me that Ronald and George formed their own team: "Too Fast, Too Furious."

Friday evening before the party, I sat on the couch with a large bowl of sliced strawberries and called George over. Bipolar children don't make transitions easily, and I wanted to prepare George for the stimulation of the party.

"Tomorrow we'll go to Toys-R-Us and buy Ronald's present. After that, we'll go to the party at the bowling alley. There will be a lot of people there, maybe even more than on Wacky Wednesdays. You ready to go?"

"Oh, yeah, Mom," he said.

The sliced strawberries felt slippery in our hands. George leaned his head back and let three slices slide through his fingers into his open mouth. "Awesome," he said, smiling at me with strawberries stuck between his teeth. George held up his hand and spread his fingers, allowing the sticky red juice to run down his palm.

I smiled. In that moment, the world consisted of just the two of us and a bowl of sweet berries. That evening, I was a great mom and George was the son of my dreams. It was a night to remember.

On Saturday morning we entered the warehouse-sized toy store. Aisles crowded with a maze of toy displays tempted us with Spiderman action figures, skateboards, and Nerf blasting guns. Rocking from one foot to the other, George wandered past shelves of toys. He stepped onto a bottom shelf while holding onto a higher shelf, sliding his feet one at a time across the bottom one, as if walking along the cliff face of a mountain. He shoved the Lego sets onto the floor with his feet.

"George, get down." I bent to replace the boxes of Legos.

As he stepped down, George grabbed several balls off the shelves, sending them bouncing in every direction. He kicked one.

"Boo-ya! Look at that go!" He grinned at me.

Dashing off, he snatched a red soccer ball and slam-dunked it into the shopping cart.

"Ronald likes red," he said.

Racing to the remote-controlled cars, he picked two, one for Ronald and another for himself. I bought George the same present as Ronald in the hope that they could play together.

Seeing how hyper he was acting in the store, I became apprehensive. How would he handle the stimulation of the bowling alley? Perhaps I'd expected too much.

"George, take deep breaths. Dial yourself down."

George stood at attention and exhaled. "Dial it down" was a cue we'd learned from the occupational therapist who works with George, teaching him how to self-regulate his moods.

George nodded his head. "Okay, Mom."

The bill totaled over fifty dollars. Focused on making George's experience successful, I paid it.

Smells of French fries, pizza, and bowling shoes rushed at me as we entered the bowling alley. Video games blared and bleeped. I held George's hand. His palms were rough and calloused from jumping ramps on his BMX bike, racing on his scooter, and digging holes in our front lawn.

"Remember, George, no jumping."

George repeated our usual litany: "No kicking. No jumping. No biting. No throwing."

Together, we walked toward the children's party at the far end of the alley, where two long tables were set with paper tablecloths, balloons, and bags of party favors for the guests.

A blonde woman wearing a blue blouse and pink pearl earrings approached us. "Hi, George. She waved at my son and smiled at me. "You must be George's mom."

Lowering herself to his height, she smiled. "George, we're so happy you've come." She took the bag of presents from me.

Who was this woman? Not Ronald's mother. I tried to identify her. "Are you Ronald's stepmother?"

Shaking her head, she said, "No. I'm his mom."

I had never seen this woman before. The sound of the bowling balls crashing against the pins banged inside my head. I blinked.

"Where's Ronald?"

"There's Ronnie."

She pointed to a group of boys. I turned, looking for Ronald, but she pointed at a huge boy with a buzz cut and red Xs spray-painted around his head. This Ronald was not George's best friend. The boy's mother turned to greet other partygoers.

Squatting in front of George, I pointed toward Ronald and whispered, "Do you know him?"

"Him? That kid? Mom, I don't even know that kid."

Thoughts collided in my mind. There must have been two boys named Ronald who bowled in the Wacky Wednesday league. I remembered my husband had said that they were passing out invitations. He must not have investigated beyond that limited piece of information and had accepted an invitation to the wrong Ronald's birthday party—a stranger's. All the assumptions I had made since I first read the card tumbled like tenpins.

I wanted to be sure. "George, do you know this Ronald?" Confused, disappointed, feeling humiliated, I still clung to my desire for success. Could this possibly still work?

George shuffled his feet and rocked his head back and forth. "Not really. I see him around." George scanned the bowling alley. "Ronald might come, Mom."

"George, Ronald's not coming. This isn't his party. I can take the presents back, and we can leave. We bought those gifts for your friend, and we can give them to him." I started to walk toward the present table. I felt like two people, one who wanted to grab the presents and run, and the other who needed to sit down on the floor and cry.

George yanked on my arm, green eyes fixed on my face. He looked around me at the kids lining up to bowl and the confetti-covered party tables.

"Mom, dial it down."

I froze in place. "Do you want to stay?"

"Why not?"

I asked him, "Are you sure?"

George tugged on my sweater, and we joined the wrong Ronald's party.

I sat in the hard plastic chair in the bowlers' seating area, while George tagged on to the end of a line of children waiting to bowl. Less than a minute passed, and he began tapping his thighs and head with his hands. Drifting out of line, he walked by me, circling. On his third pass, he lifted his hand and we high-fived each other. The other children didn't protest when he cut back into line.

This was crazy. I felt he didn't belong there. We didn't belong.

Ronald's mom came by. "You can leave George here. Take a break."

"No, I'd better stay."

"Thanks for coming." She sat beside me. "I like George. He's got a lot of heart. I was glad when his dad took one of our invitations."

He didn't know whose invitation he was picking up, I thought.

I watched George lift the bowling ball and press it against the tip of his nose. I prayed he didn't drop it on his foot or follow it down the alley, as if sliding into home base. He launched the ball and it raced toward the pins, bouncing off of the gutter bumpers once and knocking over eight pins. I exhaled. Just the simple act of George successfully casting a bowling ball down the alley felt like he'd won Olympic gold. I felt my body relax. I sank down, feeling more comfortable in the chair.

"It's hard to have parties for Ronnie," Ronald's mother continued talking. "He's hyper and rough around the edges socially. It's hard to raise a kid with special needs. I used to dread Ronnie's parties. But this one's working out."

I turned and caught her watching Ronnie standing in line, laughing with two boys his age. I understood the expression on her face.

"It's a fun party," I said, smiling. "Thanks for inviting us."

George missed the remaining two pins, spun around, and hopped past the other children to the back of the line, where he turned and thrust his two thumbs up and raised his arms above his head. A perfect day.

—Patricia Ljutic

Delilah's Not Diabetic

"I want that one," I said. The rabbit was white with a brown patch on one ear, like he had been dipped in chocolate milk. She curled up in the corner of the cage, separate from the other rabbits.

"She'll be hard work," said the man.

I could tell he thought that I was dumb, just because I was eight. He wore a checked shirt and had tried to style his hair like a pop star.

"Where's your mummy?" he asked, kneeling down to open a small door.

"She's looking at the cats," I said.

Mum likes cats, but she couldn't have one because I'm allergic to them. Rabbits are fine; they don't make me itch. She made me take one of my pills before we set off for the animal rescue home. She said it would work in time because the place was half an hour away.

"She's called Delilah," said the man.

"I know," I said. I could just tell.

He looked at me that frowny way adults always look when we know stuff. He filled the water bowl and poured pellets into another bowl. Then he locked the door with a small key.

"There you are, Katy," said Mum, appearing from around the corner.

"I was always here," I said.

"Do you see one you like?" she asked, brushing my hair behind my ear with her fingers.

I pulled it back down again. "I like Delilah," I said. "She's my rabbit."

"She's not very well," said the man. He wasn't talking to me. I could tell because he didn't talk slowly. He looked at Mum. "She has what we call 'tilt.' She fell from high up, and now she can't stand for a long time. See how her head tilts slightly?"

I could, but I didn't mind. She was my rabbit. We chose each other.

"She'll need extra exercise," said the man. "She likes to be massaged too."

"What's massaged?" I asked Mum.

"Stroked," said Mum.

"I can do that," I said.

Delilah lolloped to the center of the cage, sat up on her hind legs, and wriggled her nose. I bent down and put my finger through the bars. She was shy. She just looked at me. Mum and the man whispered; I knew they were saying that Delilah was ill.

"You like her, sweetie?" Mum asked me.

"Of course, she's my rabbit," I said. "Like you did when you picked me."

"What?" asked Mum.

She didn't remember. Adults never do.

"I have to fill out some forms," she said. I gave her a hug, because sometimes that's all mothers understand, and she kissed my forehead.

I came home from school on Wednesday, and she was there, waiting for me. Delilah. Mum had stuffed her new hutch full of hay. She had a shiny red bowl for the pellets and a bottle for water. I started to open the hutch door.

"Injection first," said Mum.

"Do I have to? I want to say hello to Delilah. You said she needs lots of stroking."

"And you need your insulin before tea."

I've had diabetes for a year. It doesn't bother me too much. The injections don't hurt anymore, but they do make me cross when I want to do something else instead.

"If you have a try at doing it yourself it might be quicker," said Mum, shaking the injection pen twenty times and screwing on the needle.

"Next time," I said.

She thinks I'm scared, but I'm not. My hand is just smaller than hers and won't work the lever as well. I was scared at the hospital when the doctors realized I was ill. They tried to put a huge needle in my arm. I wouldn't let them. They asked if I wanted to watch *Shrek*, and I told them that I wasn't stupid, that they were going to put that thing in my arm while I was laughing at Donkey. Mum was sad, I could tell. She said I could have a rabbit in the spring if I was brave.

Click. Mum injected me with insulin. I counted to ten like I always do to make sure none of it leaks out. Then she removed the syringe and put the lid back on the pen.

"Now eat your sausages, and you can go and see Delilah," she said.

After tea I went to the hutch. I opened the door, but I didn't put my hand inside. I didn't want to scare Delilah. I'd been reading about rabbits. Some are afraid of humans. They don't like to be picked up. Delilah was hunched up in the corner, her chocolatey ear flat. I walked away from the hutch and lay on the grass.

"What are you doing?" called Mum from the kitchen.

"Rabbits are curious," I called back. "They'll come if you lie down."

"Don't get mud on those new jeans," she said.

Mums never get the important stuff. Just like they don't remember anything. I closed my eyes and waited. Then I felt warm breath on my cheek. I kept very still. Delilah sniffed my arm. Slowly, I reached out to stroke her. She let me, just once, and then hopped away, falling over twice, because she's ill.

But I was very happy.

"You want to know why cats make me itch," I said to Mum at bedtime.

Why?" she asked.

"So that I'd pick Delilah," I said.

"Your banana is there, next to the bed," she said.

Why would I forget? She leaves one for me every night in case I'm hungry. She checks me, too, at about nine, when she thinks I'm asleep. But I'm not; I have too much to think about.

"All the other babies made you itch," I told her. "That's why you picked me."

Mum kissed my forehead and sniffed, like she might be getting a cold.

"Goodnight, sweetie," she said and turned off the light.

On Saturday I spent all day with Delilah. Olivia wanted me to go and play with the new Nintendo Wii at her house, but I told her that I had obligations. I have a rabbit now.

"Put your cardigan on," Mum told me. "It's chilly out there today."

How could I be chilly with Delilah on my tummy? She was getting braver every day. Today she climbed onto my chest and sat for a minute, licking her paws. I loved how one ear flopped and the other stood up, like one was tired and one was ready to play. The chocolate one was the happy one.

"Would you like carrots?" I asked her.

She ate them from my hand. Then she let me stroke her for five full minutes; it might have been longer. She was still quite shy and a bit scared, but I understood. When I came home from the hospital last year and had to start having two injections every day, I was pretty nervous. I screamed one time when Mum did it wrong. I still loved her, though.

"Do you want to try with the pen today?" Mum asked when I ran in to get my mid-afternoon snack.

"Next time," I said.

On Thursday when I came home from school, I felt grumpy. Mum tested my blood with the meter and said I needed some sugar. I ate my chocolate bar and ignored Delilah.

"She ate lots of vegetables today and let me stroke her for fifteen minutes," said Mum.

"I'm not bothered," I said.

"Did you notice her head doesn't tilt as much?"

"Delilah's not diabetic," I said. "She'll get better."

"Only with you looking after her," said Mum.

I knew that she was trying to cheer me up. I finished my chocolate and wiped the crumbs off my lap. It takes about ten minutes for the sugar to work. Then I went to Delilah's hutch. She came forward straight away and sniffed my hand. I stepped back, and she jumped onto the grass. Mum was right. Her head didn't look so strange today.

"Here, Delilah," I whispered.

She scampered around the garden. Then suddenly she leapt into the air. She twisted her body and flicked her head and feet. She landed on the grass and ran in a circle. I ran inside.

"Delilah did a binky!" I cried.

"What's a binky?" asked Mum.

"Don't you know anything?" I tutted. "It's when a rabbit jumps really high to show how happy it is."

I hugged Mum's waist and ran back outside. I did a binky too. I jumped so high that the soles of my feet smacked against my bottom. Twice.

After tea Mum got the insulin box from the cupboard. We sat in the front room where I can watch TV at the same time. *Doctor Who* was on. I'm the only girl in my class who isn't scared of it.

"Are you happy with Delilah? Did you pick the right pet?" Mum asked me.

"Oh, yes," I said.

I took the insulin pen from her. I shook it twenty times and screwed on the needle.

"Remember when I said that you picked me because I didn't make you itch?" I asked her.

"Yes," Mum said.

She watched me find the fleshiest part of my thigh but didn't try and boss me around like she sometimes does. I pierced the skin with the needle.

"Well, I'll tell you a secret," I said as I clicked the top of the pen myself. The insulin felt cold.

"What's that?" she asked, packing up the box.

"I picked you as well," I said.

Then I watched *Doctor Who* until bedtime, because it was the episode where the Daleks take over the world.

—Louise Beech

A Regular Guy

"Do you want me to come in with you while you get your haircut?"

"No," replies my nineteen-year-old son, Matthew. "I want him to think I drove here by myself."

When I suggest that he remove the junior sheriff sticker from his tee-shirt before he goes in, he refuses.

"I want him to think I take care of bad guys."

Matthew has autism and wants to be a regular guy in the worst way. But he is crippled by social awkwardness that, try as we have, we can't train out of him. Earlier in the day, we had been to the dentist, where Matthew read *The Care Bears Go to the Dentist* while waiting for his turn. To look at his face, you would think he was reading *Paradise Lost.* I sat next to him with a straight face while the packed waiting room stifled laughter. And who could blame anyone?

Most of the people in the waiting room have seen Matthew around town and wondered about him. They have seen him at the skateboard store, pretending he works there, and at the hardware store with his large hands wrapped around a bottle of weed killer, studying the label earnestly. They have seen him pushing a gas-powered lawnmower around town with a weed whacker and a leaf blower stacked on top. What is with that kid, they seem to wonder.

Matthew doesn't want just to be a regular guy. He also wants to be The Landscape Guy—the lawn-care authority and poisonous plant and weed expert of our Northern California community. He's been known to approach strangers with warnings about deadly nightshade, oleander, and water hemlock. Some snicker and walk away; others show a glimpse of understanding and stop to chat. They make his day, and I know my smile of gratitude makes theirs.

"He would be really good-looking if he didn't have autism," my twelve-year-old son says of Matthew, and as unkind as it sounds, I know what he means. Matthew is very handsome, with a tall and wiry frame, broad shoulders, and sandy blonde hair. His eyebrows arch dramatically to frame his brown eyes, and his jaw is square and masculine. But his exaggerated expressions and body carriage set him apart from the regular guys he would like to identify with. His forehead twists with intensity, he smiles too suddenly and too widely, his hungry-for-friendship gaze is desperate. He doesn't pick up on subtle social cues, like when to step back, when to change the subject from poisonous plants to anything more universal, and he doesn't understand that it is not cool to ask a girl if she has ever had a seizure. He likes to wear dark socks and sandals, shorts, and a tee-shirt that says "Shumaker Landscaping," with our phone number below. The phone number, of course, is not for soliciting business, as Matthew would like to believe, but for identification purposes.

"Is this Shumaker Landscaping? There is a man mowing my lawn, and I already have a gardener. Could you please get him to stop?"

Matthew has been attending Camphill Special School in Pennsylvania since he was sixteen, a year when adolescence fueled Matthew's already impulsive and socially inappropriate actions. He'd wander from home and school looking for "hot girls," asking them if he could touch their hair, even with their mothers present. His behavior resulted in hurt feelings, angry phone calls, and visits from the police. My husband and I came to the painful conclusion that Matthew was not safe and that he was endangering others in our community.

The good news is that now Matthew is thriving at Camphill and is an important part of its community of disabled people. He goes to class, cooks, and does his own laundry. He helps to prune trees, tend an organic garden, and take care of the grass. During the winter he shovels snow gleefully, and he has become fascinated with weather patterns in the Northeast. He brags about his newfound responsibilities and tells us he is "good at hard things." When he graduates from this school, he hopes to live in the Camphill community in Santa Cruz, California.

But he'll come home for winter breaks and spring breaks, and if you live in Lafayette and you're lucky, you might spot him walking around town with his garden tools, rain or shine, just a regular working guy. His mother is the blonde hiding behind the wheel of her Toyota Highlander or behind a bush, keeping an eye on her first-born son. Just a regular mom with a giant lump in her throat.

—Laura Shumaker

The Things I Could Not Change

For years I pretended I only had one brother. It wasn't that I didn't love Dick; it was just hard to explain a slightly retarded brother to the outside world. Within our family, he was often the axis around whom the rest of us spun. Because he relied on us so completely, I believed he was the living embodiment of our faults and successes as a family, and I was reluctant for others to see us so plainly.

Whenever I first hear the words, "Richard's in the hospital," my throat constricts. I picture my brother being ripped out of my life, leaving a ragged space in the family portrait. I tiptoe to the edge of a black hole and peer down at what would be left of my life if he were gone. And there've been many episodes—always something scary and shocking—that sent Dick to the hospital or to bed.

His first seizure occurred when he was about nineteen and I was eleven, before any of us knew he was epileptic. It was the year he finally earned his license. One morning I heard my parents talking in low tones about how Dick had driven the car into a ditch. He crawled through the broken window and up through the tall grass. Holding his sore left arm in his right hand, he walked home. Dick said he only remembered seeing a bright light and then waking up in the ditch.

With the first seizure that I witnessed, he faded into silence. "Dick, can you hear me?" I yelled into his blank face. He didn't blink or flinch. It was as if he had disappeared inside himself. Gradually, his body started drawing up, the muscles in his arms and legs tensing, his body curling around itself, elbows clinched to his side, hands clutching air. His forearms jerked, slowly at first, then picked up speed, pummeling his chest and knees like some battery-operated toy gone haywire. I sat on the floor with him, holding his wrists, saying over and over, "It's okay. You're gonna be okay."

The seizures came on more frequently each year. At first they caught us off-guard. Once, during a family vacation to Lake George, Dick was napping in his room under a low ceiling. My mother and I, reading in the living room, heard a dull thumping. After a minute or so, we decided to investigate. We found Dick curled in the fetal position on his bed, his forehead red and swelling from banging on the rafter above him.

It took months to find the proper balance of medication to stop his seizures. When the medicine was too strong, he'd sit for hours at the kitchen table, head propped in his hands, a small line of drool seeping from the corner of his mouth. I'd ask him a question, and it was as if everything inside him had slowed. I'd fidget while he rubbed his chin and stared out of cloudy gray eyes. A few minutes later, his voice would emerge, rusty from lack of use, "Uh, well . . . I think . . ." By that time, I could see he had forgotten the question or that he was no longer capable of answering it.

Eventually, the doctors were able to find a drug combination that didn't place an extra drag on Dick's mental processes. It was good to have my brother back, but even then, I'd get calls out of the blue that he was in the emergency room when a frantic teacher or friend drove him there after experiencing one of his seizures. Dick would regularly forget his medicine. One time, he must have blacked out while walking to work, because he called me from the hospital, saying he didn't know how he got there.

After each episode, I was left with a mixture of feelings: fear that my brother was so fragile, shame that my family couldn't fix his problems, and guilt that I was healthy and he was not.

The word "retarded" always seemed too strong for Dick. He was mentally handicapped due to a lack of oxygen during his birth, according to my mother. She said as a child he was just slightly behind other kids his age. Slow to learn, he could catch onto things given enough time. With repetition, he was able to learn the alphabet, basic reading skills, and enough math to eventually graduate from high school. Although, with today's standardized testing, I doubt he would have made it out of the fourth grade.

Teachers liked Dick because he tried so hard. He spent hours with his head bowed over the dining room table, my mother beside him. She patiently guided him through multiplication tables, spelling, history, geography. The rest of her kids breezed through school, making As and Bs without much effort. I remember the day Dick came home with his report card in the tenth grade, his crooked front teeth pushing against the inside of his smile.

"What are you so happy about?" I asked.

"Look, Ann!" He fumbled with his books, dropping one on the floor as he slid the report card in front of me. "I made an A!"

I glanced down at the column of grades.

History	D
Science	D
English	D
Math	D

Art	C
Gym	B
Chorus	A

My first instinct was to cringe at the number of Ds, but when I glanced up, my brother was smiling so hard it hurt to look at him. "That's great, Dick."

My mother often said Dick and I were alike. I assumed she meant the same light-brown hair color, the same tall and lanky builds, and the same pale skin, because in some very big ways, we were opposites. He was a boy; I was a girl. He was retarded, and I was labeled as "bright" by my teachers. But even with these differences, my brother and I shared a childhood.

I counted on him to enjoy the excitement of Christmas with me. As my other siblings grew bored with stockings and early Christmas mornings, I could always creep into Dick's room at 4:00 or 5:00 A.M. and whisper something like "Ho! Ho! Ho!" He'd be up in a flash and down the stairs with me to see what Santa had brought. We'd sit on the couch together and open our stockings. He'd pull each item out one at a time, examining it so carefully and slowly that he made the magic of Christmas go on and on . . . until I outgrew the desire to wake up early Christmas morning.

As a teenager, I became acutely aware of how different Dick was from other people. With our age difference, most of my friends didn't know he existed until they came home to spend the night with me. I'd try to walk around him in the living room without making eye contact with him, in hopes that my friends would do the same thing. Too often they'd stop and stare as he rocked on the couch, thumb in his mouth, hair sticking up at odd angles all over his head.

"He's mildly retarded," I'd whisper in the privacy of my room.

They'd cock their head as if wanting to know more, but I'd always let the subject drop.

Sometimes, when the family went out for dinner, I'd comb his hair or send him back to the bathroom to shave again because he missed a spot. There was a period when I even tried to dress him, picked out shirts that brought out the blue in his eyes, pants that were the right length. But somehow there was always something wrong. His zipper was only halfway up, he'd missed loops with his belt, or his pants were pulled up unnaturally high around his waist.

Even if I'd been able to fix these things, I knew I could never change the way he walked—the way his chin jutted out in front of him, one hand swinging by his side, the other jammed in his pocket. I could never speed up the long pauses when someone asked him a question. I couldn't change his answers that never quite matched the questions.

"Mildly retarded" was the phrase my mother used. I guess it was her way of recognizing that he was different, without offending my father, who talked as if Dick had the exact same abilities as the rest of his children. Mom said Daddy had a blind spot where Dick was concerned. She thought it was because he identified so strongly with him. Although Dick was their second child, my father had been in Korea when my sister was born. He'd been granted leave for my brother's birth, and he gave him the name Richard in honor of his beloved oldest brother.

My father bestowed gifts on Dick from the beginning. I remember photos of my brother lying in a crib beside a football. His tiny arms waved over a scrawny body. Dick was a breech baby, which added to the complications during his birth. My mother said Dick was blue when he came out and that he spent the first six weeks of his life in an incubator. Having faced the reality of death during war time, my father must have bonded in a special way to his young son. Not known for his patience, he spent endless hours grooving Dick's golf swing, teaching him how to bowl and play tennis. I picture his large hands guiding Dick's finer ones over and over.

Bowling became the sport of choice for our family outings. Dick, dressed in jeans and a bowling shirt tucked in the front of his pants, brought his own pale-gray shoes, his own bag, and a black ball with yellow sparkles on it drilled to fit his slim fingers. My father coached Dick on the basics—step, step, step, slide one foot behind the other, release, hand follows through in the air. My brother got so good at it that he had his own style, a real flair. Sometimes, when he released the ball, his thumb popped out of the hole with a *thonk* and the ball rose in the air in an arc and came down on the lane with a bang. I'd hold my breath as the sparkles blurred and the ball curved from the side arrow right into the pocket that sent the pins tumbling.

Later, when Dick and I bowled on a league, everyone wanted him on their team. Dick could pull a losing team into contention with a couple of strikes. And, like a concealed weapon, he always surprised his opponents. Members of the other team shifted their eyes when he sat down, said hello at the most, maybe shook his hand. Not another word to either of us was uttered until Dick picked up an impossible split, nicking the right pin and sliding it into the left one. Suddenly, there were looks exchanged. They'd say things like, "Did I see what I thought I saw?" or "Where'd you find him? This guy's amazing." Dick always responded with a huge smile, an awkward offering of his hand for someone to shake, and the hope that one of these people would turn into a friend.

When I hear Dick is in the hospital, an image of him at the bowling alley flashes through my mind. As a teenager, it was the one place where I was proud he was my brother. I think of his rows of trophies—wobbly metal bowlers poised on top of wooden bases, some with broken appendages or missing heads—gathering dust on his bureau. The ones he won as a kid are stacked up against the ones he continues to win as an adult. A few years ago, I tried to get him to throw some of them away, at least the broken ones. I'm glad he didn't.

—*Ann Campanella*

He's Fine

"He's fine."

That's what husbands will say.

That's what the father is apt to say when you, the mother, raise a concern about your precious, perfect child.

And so you spend some time in limbo, going back and forth between your husband's practical thinking and your maternal instincts. Eventually, your maternal instincts take over.

But from the moment you notice a "problem" and get that sinking feeling that "something's wrong"—that's when the journey begins. It starts with a sense of mild concern that coasts to a state of deep concern that accelerates to a steady pulse of utter panic. Anxiety consumes you like a bad virus. You go through your day, go through the motions, putting on a happy face, engaging in chit-chat, acting like you're actually interested in your friend's new car. But lurking inside you is a gray, dense fog and a voice, your own voice, shouting, *Something's wrong! Something's wrong! Something's wrong!*

My son was three when I noticed a language problem. He would repeat, verbatim, any question posed to him.

"How are you?"

Response: "How are you."

"Did you have a good day?"

Response: "Did you have a good day."

"What would you like for lunch?"

Response: "What would you like . . ."

You get the picture.

The words were there. The speech was there. Enunciation was pretty darn clear too. But there was no "yes" or "no" or answer to a question asked. Just an echo.

Echolalia.

That's what it's called. Echolalia. Instead of getting an appropriate answer from your child, you just get back what you threw out. For a time, it's almost humorous, like an extended game of telephone, in which a sentence is passed along from one person to another. But then panic kicks in and the fun stops.

Meanwhile, you listen to your husband tell you "he's fine." And you go through your days, day after day, with your own questions echoing in your ears. As one month gives way to another and then another, your maternal instincts keep echoing in your head, *Something's wrong.* So you annoy your husband with your own echo, "Are you sure he's okay?"

"He's fine."

You listen to your husband. You trust his judgment because he's a smart guy. And you make sure to keep that smile on your face . . . until one day your mother—who never says anything negative about the precious, perfect child—says something to the tune of, "Yes, I think something is wrong."

Your smile fades. The façade drops away. And the gray fog inside gets a little darker, a bit denser.

Then you begin your journey through the fog—to the phone, to the library, to the Internet, to the doctor's office, to the climactic Evaluation.

You get your calendar and schedule the big event and moment of truth.

Then you pray. You get down on your knees and pray good prayers that you know God hears.

And it was only after dropping to those knees that I had the courage to set up the evaluation. And there on my knees I wanted to stay.

There on my knees I learned to love, to accept, and to become strong in the midst of the fog. When you set off on your journey with strength, you can face the long struggle head on.

Of course, you are not alone in your struggle, not alone in your journey. The precious, perfect child must make the journey as well. He, too, must step up to the plate and gather up his strength.

Then, early in the journey, a sign is given. For me, it was a sign. I wasn't looking for a sign, but it happened, and I took it as one. And I don't doubt it was a sign, and I don't doubt that signs lead to miracles. Miracles like new therapies and technologies that answer specific prayers.

Here's what happened:

We got the diagnosis: auditory processing delay. We got the plan: speech therapy and Fast Forword (an amazing program, by the way).

And then, more prayers. I put aside my pride. That nasty pride that makes me want to show off and pretend I'm not who I am. That shameful pride that makes me embarrassed of my loved ones. I put aside the pride and the selfishness, so that I was just "a mom on her knees" asking for help and mercy and guidance.

So early one morning, early in the journey, with worn out, cried out, red eyes, I got up from my knees and walked into the backyard, where my beautiful boy crouched in his sandbox, shovel in hand, playing happily, as my never-worried, "he's fine" husband strummed a guitar in a hammock.

Then I sneezed.

And the precious, perfect child looked up and said, "God bless you, Mommy."

A response. Not an echo. A perfect response. A perfect, miraculous response.

It would be really cool to end the story here, but there's a bit more.

We spent two summers doing the Fast Forword program. It was expensive and time-consuming. But now my language-challenged toddler is a talkative, musically gifted, friendly, baseball-playing little boy. The delay in auditory processing was just that—a delay.

And now, the word "delay" has taken on a whole new meaning for me.

Why is it that, in hindsight, we see more clearly?

At three, my son would play, laugh, do puzzles in a flash, and play songs on the piano. Yet, I focused only on his language delay—meanwhile, delaying my enjoyment of him, just as he was.

I wish I hadn't been so focused on what was "wrong" that I overlooked all that was perfectly "fine." I wish I could take back the days I spent drowning in worry and could spend that time, instead, just experiencing my precious, almost-perfect child. I wish I had seen then what I see now.

None of us is perfect. My son needed help with language. That's all. He wasn't missing a thing. But I was. I was so hung up on the negatives that I missed out on far too many positives—all the adorable, remarkable things that should have been the highlight of every day.

So now, in hindsight, having made my way through the fog, I finally get it: Embrace the positive. Embrace the delay. Give me a delay, any time. Let me slow down and "lie down in green pastures." Let me enjoy these precious, perfect days that go by so fast.

—*Mary* C. M. *Phillips*

The Greatest Gift

My daughter Jaimie is my miracle girl. With a bicornuate uterus and having had cervical cancer, I was told I would probably not be able to conceive, and that if I did, the odds were I wouldn't be able to carry to term. But after three years of trying, I did get pregnant, and although I almost lost the baby several times during the pregnancy and the birth was difficult, I gave birth to the first of four beautiful children.

As a newborn, Jaimie reminded me of one of those babies in photos from the early 1900s: big, blue, wonder-filled eyes; poker-straight, strawberry-blonde hair, and creamy, porcelain-doll skin. As I'd stand over her crib and watch her sleep, my heart would fill with a pure love I didn't know existed before she did. But as Jaimie grew, we noticed that she struggled with her environment and the people in it. When Jaimie was two and a half, we learned that our miracle girl had sensory processing disorder (SPD).

Most people have a natural ability to tune out unnecessary sights, smells, sounds, and other sensations so that they can focus. Jaimie lacks this filtering ability. Her sensory organs receive and transmit messages to her brain, but her brain doesn't understand how to read those messages. This leaves her overwhelmed and confused a great deal of the time. Her fear of being over-stimulated in any way also prevents her from feeling comfortable in certain situations and places or with new people.

Jaimie struggles with many sensory sensitivities, but her most severe is tactile, the sense of touch. From the age of about six months old, she rejected any form of light touch, even when offered in comfort and especially from her father. As parents, Steve and I have found this to be the most excruciating part of coping with SPD. I've longed to wrap my arms around my daughter and to feel her tiny arms around me. But Jaimie has never been able to express her love for me in this way—not because she doesn't love me, but because such physical contact is excruciating for her. Even asking Jaimie for a hug upsets her terribly. So Jaimie "hugs" by leaning her head toward me until it barely touches me, ever so briefly, and saying "hug." I've come to accept and appreciate this expression of Jaimie's love. But deep in my heart, I wish and hope for an honest-to-goodness hug.

Shortly after Jaimie received her SPD diagnosis, she began therapy to learn how to communicate with us more effectively. Steve and I were actively involved in her therapy so that we could help her at home. For Steve, it was also a way to finally bond with the daughter he'd been able to love only from a distance. More than anything, I was grateful to finally have a name for the unknown, unseen assailant we'd been fighting since Jaimie's birth.

It wasn't an easy road; Jaimie had a real problem with anyone coming into her sacred world of routine and organization. But after a year of therapy, I saw positive changes in her little personality as she slowly allowed people in. Perhaps she felt there were now people in her life other than me who understood what she was feeling inside and who liked her anyway. Jaimie began to express in words what had been trapped in her mind. Yet, despite the positive aspects of her therapy, she still refused to be touched and would become very distressed if we so much as talked about hugs. So I simply waited with my arms ready.

One evening when Jaimie was three years old, Steve made me an offer I couldn't refuse. "Hon, why don't you go out for a walk and let me hang out with Jaimie."

Jaimie had been doing so well with her therapy that I thought, *Let's give it a shot!*

It would be the first time I'd gone anywhere without Jaimie since she was born. I hesitated, because Steve didn't always do things exactly the way Jaimie needed them to be done and didn't always have the patience for her strict routines, which caused Jaimie to explode in frustration. Still, she had to learn to trust him and to be comfortable with him. What if, God forbid, something happened to me? All she'd have left would be Steve.

So I got ready to go and then went to say goodbye to Jaimie. I found her coloring at the kitchen table.

"Jaimie, Mama is going for a short walk, but I'll be back soon." I said. "You and Daddy can color until I get back, okay?"

As I spoke, Jaimie seemed not to hear me, but her coloring got slower and she ground her crayon into the page. Worried, I looked at Steve, who kissed me on the forehead as he gently pushed me to the door.

"We'll be fine," he said. "It's only for twenty minutes or so. No worries."

As I walked down the stairs, I fought a wave of guilt pulling me back into the house. But after a few minutes in the fresh air, I felt exhilarated. *So this is what it feels like to do my own thing*, I thought.

Given that I couldn't even use the bathroom without leaving the door open because Jaimie needed to know where I was all the time, that walk was like going to a party for me. It was the best twenty minutes of my life.

Nearing the house on my return home, I heard what I thought were crow screeches. I quickly realized it was Jaimie.

I flew up the front stairs, fumbled with my keys in the lock, and found Steve straddling Jaimie on the floor, holding her arms and legs so she wouldn't hurt him or herself as she screamed. "No! I don't like you. I want Mama."

Steve heard my sneakers squeak across the linoleum and looked up at me like a doctor losing his patient. I cupped his chin, then dropped to the floor. He enveloped my hand in his and placed it on top of Jaimie's chest. After Steve left the room, I carefully lifted Jaimie off the floor and squeezed her to me (she calmed better with deep touch), holding her tight as the front of my shirt soaked up her tears, sweat, and drool.

For more than two hours, I tried every technique I'd been taught to calm Jaimie, but nothing worked. Finally, I had no choice but to put her in her bed, so she could release the rest of her fit in privacy. I went to the solitude of my room, flopped on the bed like a rag doll, and allowed myself to do something I hadn't done for a long time: I cried. I didn't stop the tears from coming like I usually did; I just let them flow.

I cried because I was angry that my daughter had SPD. Because I felt scared and frustrated and helpless that I couldn't help her and didn't know what I was supposed to do. Because I lost my temper with her when she wouldn't stop crying. Because I felt guilty about wishing she was "normal." Mostly, I cried for Jaimie, because she knew she was different but didn't understand why. Why couldn't she let us reach her? Why couldn't her mommy help her?

When I finally stopped, drained after my emotional release, I heard Jaimie downstairs with Steve. I splashed cold water on my face in a feeble attempt to reduce the redness in my eyes and then went to join my family. As I descended the stairs, I thought of the love that shone in Jaimie's big blue eyes, reflecting the affection she so desperately wanted to give but her body simply wouldn't allow her to. Someday, I assured myself, I'd reach my daughter and she'd trust me enough to show her love for me.

I entered the living room, where Jaimie and Steve watched a movie.

"Can I join you guys?" I asked.

At the sound of my voice, Jaimie jumped up and ran to me. "Mama!" she cried happily.

I crouched down so she could touch my leg with her head, but instead she wrapped her tiny arms around me and hugged me—a real hug. I was in such shock it took me a few seconds to hug her back. As I wrapped my arms around her small body, she whispered, "I love you, Mama."

"Oh, Jaimie," I whispered back, "I love you too. So very much."

For the first time in my daughter's young life, I felt the same joy other mommies feel when their children express their love with a gentle embrace.

Her hug lasted for only a few seconds, but even as she pushed away from me to finish watching her movie, I still felt the warmth of her arms around me. I knew it would be a long time before she'd hug again, but I wasn't sad. Her hug was a sign of good things to come, and it renewed my hope.

Thank you, Jaimie, for your precious gift. I will treasure it always.

—Chynna Tamara Laird

The Gorilla Wore Roller Skates

Most children would say that Christmas was their favorite holiday. Our daughter Michele, however, loved Halloween and always looked forward to planning each year's costume.

Michele was born with spinal muscular atrophy, or Werdnig-Hoffman's disease, a form of muscular dystrophy, and she used a wheelchair all her life. But despite her disability, Michele was always right in the middle of the action—a real social butterfly—even on the terrace of our university housing apartment at Michigan State University, where she interacted daily with students from a number of countries when her dad was in graduate school.

We'd moved to the area that summer, and by late October with her favorite holiday fast approaching, we still didn't know many people. When Michele discovered that the local mall hosted a community

Halloween party, the wheels in her head started turning. She made a list of what she needed: black trash bags, scissors, masking tape, sunglasses, two very large sheets of poster board, and markers.

"Who are you going to be?" her father asked as we surveyed her materials.

"The Fonz," Michele said, referring to the coolest guy on television at the time, one of the stars of *Happy Days*.

The black bags were to be cut and then taped to form shiny pants, boots, and a simulated leather jacket. The wheelchair posed a unique problem, but Michele had it all figured out. Once she'd completed her art project, the poster board, fastened to the sides, transformed the chair into a motorcycle.

The big night finally arrived, and Michele's excitement was contagious. She knew that prizes would be awarded to some children. I was proud of her original costume, but as I expected, the mall was wall-to-wall ghosts and ghoulies vying for the few prizes. The action appeared to be in a central area—with a glaringly nonaccessible dip—so we could only watch from behind a crowd of kids and their parents.

Before the designated prize-announcing time, we noticed some adult-sized characters roaming the area and passing out treats and entry numbers to kids. Michele was particularly intrigued with the roller-skating gorilla. (I was, too. He must have been sweltering in that suit.) He had the warmest eyes, for an ape, and kept skating by and flirting with Michele. He was a mute gorilla, but each time he approached, Michele gave him the Fonzie "Ayyyy" she'd been practicing. He gestured his approval and gave her a quick, hairy hug. Then he skated on.

Soon, a voice on a loudspeaker said winners would be announced. Everyone surged forward. At the back of the crowd, Michele and I strained to hear as the first numbers were called. I worried about how Michele would handle the disappointment after all her planning, because from our position, she could not even see or be seen by judges.

Just then, I noticed a big, furry black figure hand something to the announcer, and another number was read. I waited for it to be repeated, just to be sure.

"Honey, that's you!" I told the excited child next to me. "The gorilla chose you."

It took some doing, but we managed to wheel our way to the judging area to accept her prize, backing the chair down some steps along the way. There, the gorilla did a little jig on his skates for the grinning Fonz as he handed her the gift-wrapped prize.

Many years have passed since that night in the mall, and we relocated a few more times during Michele's childhood. But that Halloween incident in the Midwest will always stand out in my mind. We lost Michele just after her eleventh birthday, in 1982. She was a determined child who never let her disability stand in the way of her personhood, and, despite her youth, she made a point of advocating for the disabled.

I think I know now why Halloween was so important to Michele. And it had nothing to do with tricks or treats. If all the candy had been taken away, she wouldn't have cared. It was the annual ritual of designing and dressing up in creative disguises that appealed to Michele. Halloween allowed her a needed respite from her physical limitations and gave Michele the chance to be someone else—whether it was a princess from a favorite cartoon or Underdog or one of the childhood heroes she'd portrayed. And for one magic night in an Iowa mall, she wasn't a child confined to a wheelchair. She was "the Fonz"—fearless and formidable—riding tall on a motorcycle for everyone to see, thanks to a compassionate gorilla on roller skates.

—Deb Wuethrich

This story first appeared in Buffalo Magazine, *October 22, 1992.*

Invisible Child

I'm not sure why the ability to speak is so paramount in defining our humanity. When children meet my thirteen-year-old daughter Sophie for the first time, or for that matter, when children who have known her all their lives are around us, they ask, "Why can't she talk?" When I answer that she has something in her brain that makes it difficult to learn and to talk but that she can understand you and you should just say hello and talk to her, the child who asked the question usually thinks about that for a moment, looks blankly at Sophie, and then runs off to play.

When people ask me what Sophie understands, I like to say, "Everything, I think," but I am actually not certain. Without language, her personality is blurry, and I am hard put to describe what sort of person she is. My sons, ages seven and ten, have bursting personalities. Henry is full of joy and little-boy energy; his head sweats profusely when he plays and often when he sleeps. He is earnest and speaks sweetly, and he wishes for race cars and chocolate every day. He loves to win but doesn't mind when he loses. He is unashamedly affectionate, generous in his hugs. Oliver, on the other hand, refuses to be agreeable, even when he knows it's in his best interest. He throws around language like weaponry, unafraid to voice anything. He is quiet only with a thumb in his mouth, sucking furiously but still content.

Sophie, on the other hand, can't be defined by her spoken language. She loves to look up at trees, entranced by their swaying movements. She loves to look up at ceiling fans, but she isn't mesmerized by them, she just enjoys them. I know this, because she looks away, back to me, to her food, to something else in the room. She loves to pick up toys that vibrate and hold them to her cheek or in her mouth, seeking sensory input, I suppose, added sensation.

I'm not sure what sensation she has left. I'm not sure what pathways for sensation in her brain have managed to survive the tens of thousands of seizures she has experienced and the potent anti-seizure medications that she took for many years.

She is insistent on going outside, almost all the time. She'll lead you to the door wherever she is and stand in front of it, waiting, until you open it and lead her out. When I lift her out of the car and put her on her feet, she'll turn away from the house and pull me toward the sidewalk or the grass so that she can stay outside. But she never uses words to make her demands.

At the beach, when she sees the ocean off in the distance, she begins what seems like a magnetized pull across the sand toward the water. We laugh. We say the ocean is her home, that she's a "selkie," a mermaid, that she remembers some kind of freedom and a better life in the sea.

When I get frustrated with Sophie, when she has so many little seizures that I snap and think, insanely, that she's causing them herself, I sometimes grab her too insistently and say, "Stop. Please." But it is I who stops, because her eyes look at me and tell me otherwise. It is the seizures that control her.

Whenever we get home from a trip, we bring Sophie to her room. She walks in and heads straight for her bed, a box spring and mattress on the floor. This is one of the many accommodations that we've made for her safety, and the low bed enables her to sit by herself and even roll off when she wants. She sits down and pulls her legs up, Indian-style, simultaneously swiveling her hips and scooting sideways and forward until she's sitting completely on the bed. This movement is always exactly the same, a language of relief and comfort. Once, when we had been away for two weeks and she walked down the hall to her room and saw it, yellow and lavender, the carpet thick and shaggy, the three windows filtering sunlight, she smiled a real smile, wide and joyful and happy.

My extended family lives all over the East Coast, and being thousands of miles away from us seems to make them even less familiar with Sophie than those curious children who ask about her inability to speak. Although my parents and sisters provide financial and emotional support, it seems to me that when we're all together, Sophie is an invisible child for the most part. She can sit in her handicapped stroller among a roomful of people for hours and no one really notices her. Her cousins will run back and forth on their way to the pool, to the beach, to ride bikes, to throw balls outside, or to grab popsicles out of the freezer. Sophie sits alone amidst all this commotion swirling around her. She might shift in her chair, cross her legs or uncross them, but no one pays any attention to her. She might murmur her customary "mmmm" as her eyes follow the activity, but she does not speak. I can't blame my nieces and nephews, my sisters, my parents, or anyone, for that matter, for not noticing Sophie.

Sometimes, they actually do notice her, and I'm sure it's painful . . . because it reminds them of something impossible to understand.

It's also easy not to talk to someone who can't talk back. I know that my family loves Sophie on some level. My mother, especially, is filled with love for her. I know that Mom loves Sophie's face, her curls, her sweetness and grace. My father, too, accepts her, and has been undyingly supportive and positive over all the years of her struggles. He rejoices in her achievements, however small. He strokes her face, leans over her and kisses her. But on another level, I suspect that both my parents don't really think of Sophie as a whole person. And I suspect that comes from her lack of language, her inability to reflect back onto others, to define herself in ways that others can understand.

Several years ago, I took Sophie in for another appointment with the head of genetics at UCLA Medical Center. Sophie had been diagnosed a few months before with yet another rare seizure disorder called "electrical status epilepticus in slow-wave sleep," and while the condition was resolved, she continued to have difficulty swallowing and eating and was losing a lot of weight. I was on one of my many manic rounds of trying to figure out what was wrong with her. Although I knew, deep down, that we'd explored every possible diagnosis and tried every available treatment out there, I wanted—I needed—for Dr. K to confirm that. I thought, desperately, that maybe researchers had discovered something new, perhaps a new metabolic or mitochondrial disorder, that Sophie could be tested for. Besides, I liked Dr. K because he seemed so intellectual. During one visit I had even discussed the Danish philosopher Kierkegaard with him. He is older, probably close to retirement, tall and thin, and wears enormous black-framed spectacles. His lab coat is always buttoned, and he's clean and old-fashioned.

When Dr. K walked into the examining office that afternoon, he had a group of students, interns, and residents with him, six or so young people. Everyone had clipboards and nodded politely at me. They all seemed to have glossy hair.

After we exchanged some pleasantries, I explained what Sophie had been going through recently and why I was there, adding with a hopeful laugh that maybe he might tell me something new.

Dr. K turned toward his students who were arranged in various casual poses around the tiny room. "See what a disaster this kid is," he said and gestured toward Sophie, who was sitting in her stroller/wheelchair, silent. "This is what can happen when seizures are uncontrolled," he finished and turned back toward me.

I was sitting on one of those horrible gray folding chairs that are found in examining rooms of teaching hospitals everywhere. I had been sitting in just such a chair, nursing Sophie, when she had been diagnosed with epilepsy at three months of age. I'd shifted in the chair then, and I shifted in the chair now. Instinctively, I grabbed the handle of Sophie's stroller with one hand and placed my other hand somewhere on her, to protect her.

But the words were out.

Disaster, he'd said. And the young, glossy-haired students had nodded, as if with confidence or maybe curiosity, anxious to learn or maybe even scared shitless.

Disaster.

Sophie might as well be invisible, is what I thought.

Something clicked shut inside me, at least toward Dr. K, whom I had liked, even admired, until that moment. I'd like to say that I protested, that I told him and his posse how little he understood anything, really. I'd like to say that I educated those people right there and then, by insisting that Sophie's life was not a disaster but a feast. That, despite her tens of thousands of seizures, her inability to move properly, to express herself, to read or write, or to reason normally,

Sophie was a person and her life was full of richness. That many people loved her, some who barely knew her. That she had two adoring brothers and an extended family of grandparents and aunts and uncles and cousins who loved and valued her, even if they didn't fully understand her and sometimes ignored her. That her babysitters were certain she was special, "from God," they said, and that they were honored to care for her. I'd like to say that I told them that Sophie loved the beach and walking outside and music, especially the guitar and piano, and that as a chef's daughter, she truly enjoyed good food. That she went to school every day, where the community around her rejoiced at her small achievements and where she was faithfully helped by an aide and dedicated teachers.

But I didn't say any of those things. Instead, those stormy thoughts raged inside me as I left the clinic and, weeping in frustration, drove home through the traffic.

Ever sensitive to whatever Sophie might understand—from spoken words to voice tone, to facial expressions, to laughter and tears, down to the changed energy in the air—I reassured her that everything was going to be all right. I told her that I was sorry I couldn't help her more. That I loved her, that so many people loved her, and that Dr. K's remarks were really just stupid.

In retrospect, although I will never consider Sophie or her life to be a disaster, I can understand why some people might think otherwise. In the world of Western medicine, Sophie is defined by her symptoms, which, because they are, as of today, uncontrolled and incurable and not understood, make her into a disaster. And in our society, being unable to speak, to verbalize one's thoughts and feelings, is considered by many to be abnormal and by some to be a disaster. When I think about all this objectively, it's understandable that most children leave her alone when they find out she can't talk. Even Sophie's brothers need encouragement to interact with her sometimes. But to overlook her because they can't hear her? To assume she understands little or nothing simply because she cannot speak words? No one—not the doctors and specialists, not her teachers and caregivers, not even her family—really knows all that Sophie does and does not understand, all that goes on inside of her that she cannot express in words.

I'm not sure what to do about this, really, how to bridge the enormous gap between who Sophie is and how she appears. Without her being able to actually tell me, I'm not sure myself what she experiences and understands. But I like to assume it's everything, just in case she does.

—Elizabeth Aquino

Super–Model Mom

I remember as a child thinking that the age of thirty was ancient. So on my mother's thirtieth birthday, I kindly reminded her to make sure all of her affairs were in order, because I was too young to try to straighten them all out myself after she was gone. When she looked at me, somewhat puzzled, I clarified. At her age, she was likely to die soon, right? I watched my sweet mother's face turn colors I didn't know skin could turn while she gritted her teeth so hard that I thought her jaw would crumble, and then she burst into tears. Sobbing hysterically, she told me that one day I would have wonderful kids to make me feel good about myself too and thanked me for being so mean on her birthday. I was truly confused. I wasn't being mean; I was trying to be a good daughter, to be mature and responsible, to make sure everything was in order before she croaked. On the eve of her thirtieth birthday, it seemed to be a natural conversation to have.

Fast-forward about eighteen years, and things began to clear up for me. I have a son with Asperger's syndrome. He doesn't always understand what is and isn't inappropriate to say. He doesn't understand that sometimes, some things are better left unsaid. On a quite regular basis, he says something that takes every ounce of patience and self-control I can muster to either ignore or respond to calmly.

One night, my then eight-year-old son and I were watching television together. Flipping through the channels, we stopped for a moment on one of those plastic surgery makeover shows. I don't really like those types of shows, but I was drawn to it like a moth to a flame. I mean, wouldn't it be nice to have larger breasts? Just a tiny bit larger? No . . . beauty comes from within, I admonished myself. And I should instill that on all my children, especially my three daughters. The opportunity presented itself right then. Before I could state my case, though, my son commented on how pretty the woman featured in the episode was after her surgery. In my most motherly tone, I told him that true beauty comes from inside.

As I began surfing the channels for something more appropriate for our family to watch, he said "Mom, you could be a super–model."

Aww, I thought, *my son thinks I'm beautiful.* My chest swelled with motherly pride and womanly vanity. I almost choked up with happiness at the expression of love and admiration flowing from my son's mouth. Almost. Until he continued . . .

"Mom, it's obvious. All you would need is a plastic surgeon to give you some skin surfaces and breast augmentation. Then, Mom, I just know that I would have the most beautiful mom in my whole school. Even prettier than Jason's mom. I swear. For real."

Wow. I was completely dumbfounded. How does a mother respond to something that sincere and . . . well, horrifying? My sweet, straightforward son, who I had always assumed thought I was already the most beautiful mother ever, thought I should have plastic surgery to be beautiful.

"Thank you," I choked out and shut off the television. It was time for me to get some beauty sleep. Evidently, I needed it. I resolved to put it out of my mind and move on.

The next day, on our way to do the grocery shopping, we stopped at a convenience store to get gasoline. While checking out his Dr. Pepper and Snickers, my son told the clerk that it would be my birthday soon.

"Really?" the clerk asked my son. "And how old will your pretty little mother be on her birthday?" I cringed at the condescending tone with which he said "pretty little mother" but smiled anyway.

I imagined my son saying, "No, no, not my pretty mother. This one."

However, without hesitation, my son answered very confidently that I would be about sixty-five or sixty-six, he thought, but wasn't completely sure.

Biting my lip, I proceeded to usher my ever-so-thoughtful son toward the door and my ever-so-persistent anger out of my head. The store clerk (a real charmer of a man) asked me if perhaps he should re-ring my purchase to give me the senior citizens' discount, after which he began to laugh uncontrollably. I mustered my most wicked ugly glare and aimed it directly at him before turning on my heel to stalk out in a decided huff.

When I slammed the car door shut, my son must have realized that I was upset. Thinking I was upset about my newly discovered old age, he told me not to worry about how old I had gotten, because even though I was so old, I didn't look a day over forty-five. He leaned over and gave me a big sincere hug and kiss, then leaned back, very pleased with himself for his thoughtfulness. What a lovely early twenty-eighth birthday present: my son making a genuine (if somewhat misguided) attempt to be thoughtful and complimentary. My fury dissolved as I realized that, even though I was not raising a good judge of age, I was raising a thoughtful, if very up-front, son.

Just then, my mind flashed back to that fateful day when my mother hissed her vehement wishes that I would have kids just like me. Finally, I understood where her anger had come from. But I also understood in that moment where her forgiveness had come from and that it had always been more forthcoming than her anger. I realized that my being secure in my mother's love and acceptance—secure enough to tell her what I was thinking—was more important to her than petty things like age and beauty. Who knew how important that lesson would be to me as the mother of a son whose social filter doesn't always work properly?

So, okay, I might not be a super–model mom, but I could still be a super mom. I gave my son a hug, and for once, a genuine "thank you."

—Mona Rigdon

This story first appeared in eparent.com, December 2007.

Different on the Outside

"Look, Ron, he has your big nose and serious expression," my wife Peggy said as she cuddled our newborn son in her arms.

But that's where Matthew's resemblance to me ended. When we peeled back the blanket, we saw again what the doctors and nurses at the hospital were so concerned about. Matt's hands were near his shoulders and his legs were abnormally short. Our baby was a dwarf.

Neither Peggy nor I had dwarfism in our families. We learned it was a genetic mix-up and could happen to anyone, but that didn't make it any easier. Not only would Matt have to deal with the challenges of dwarfism, but he also had severe physical disabilities. He'd have to endure numerous operations and endless pain, and he would always be "different."

I knew a lot about being different. At six years old, when my mom and dad divorced, I was sent to live in the country with an alcoholic uncle. I tried to stay out of his way, but everything I did got on his nerves and he'd slap me around. When he was in a drunken rage, he'd beat me brutally.

One day, after I'd been at my uncle's for a few months, my mother showed up unexpectedly at the little wooden building where I went to school. She told me she was moving away for good.

"Take me with you," I begged.

"I can't do that," she said.

I clung desperately to her skirt as she climbed the steps of the waiting bus. She pulled away and never looked back. I sat crying in the dusty road, wondering why she didn't love me.

Six months later, I was reunited with my brother and sister at my dad's home with his new wife. Scrawny and wheezing from asthma, I started second grade wearing worn-out bib overalls. The city kids teased me mercilessly, and one day I picked up a branch and whaled away on the biggest bully I could find. They finally stopped messing with me.

While in high school, I met Peggy. She saw through my rough exterior. After a stint in college and a tour of duty in the Marines, I married my sweetheart and then took a job as a trucker. I was on the road a lot, so the heavy load of raising the kids fell to her. When Matt was born, she had her hands full taking care of him and our toddler Ruth, but she still managed to take Matt to therapy, where they worked to uncurl his fingers and straighten his feet.

One day Peggy came home and said, "How is he ever going to hold a pencil, cut with scissors, or use a typewriter? Is he ever going to walk?"

I took her in my arms and consoled her, but inside I had those same fears.

Three years later, after being assured we would never have another child with dwarfism, we had Joshua. Born without a pulmonary artery, he was not expected to survive long enough to even go home. Joshua surprised us all and lived, but he needed constant care. After Joshua was born, we used birth control, but it didn't work. Two years later, we were expecting again. This time, we thought for sure we would have another healthy girl, but Sam was born with the same dwarfism as Matthew.

What I hated most was when people stared. I'd stare right back.

"Stop it, Ron," Peggy would admonish me.

"But do you see them staring at us?"

"Just look straight ahead and don't pay attention to them," she'd say.

"I just want to knock their blocks off when they look at our kids that way."

I know I was difficult to deal with, and Peggy did her best to reel me in. I had a hot temper and often flared up at the injustices I felt the world was loading on us. Many nights, in the quiet stillness, I would cry out to God. *Why can't the world see that they're little people on the outside but the same as everyone else on the inside?*

Peggy relied on the comfort of prayer. Her faith never wavered. "God will get us through," she'd often say. She was my soft place to land when the world seemed to be closing in on me.

Early on, I explained to Matt and Sam that they had dwarfism and had to learn to live with it. And I would have to live with it too. It was difficult for them and for me, but I would never walk away.

School was an especially vulnerable place for them. Matt came home from school one day and said, "Dad, I can't wear the gym shorts. They don't fit."

So I went to see the instructor, who happened to be an ex-Marine, like me, and he started to tell me about the rules. I stopped him in a hurry.

"Matt is doing the best he can to abide by your rules, but he needs to wear something appropriate for his size." I got up in his face. "We're going to get him shorts that fit. And that's the way it's going to be."

Though I won that battle for Matt, I wondered how my son would deal with other issues in the future when I wasn't there to fight for him.

We treated our sons like "normal" boys as much as we could. We even took them skiing one year, and wouldn't you know it, Sam fell and broke both of his legs. We rushed him to a hospital, and then Peggy took him to our regular doctor when we got home.

"Ron," Peggy said when she entered the house after that visit, "the first thing the doctor said was 'So what's this I hear about Sam breaking his legs skiing?' I wanted to crawl into a hole, but then he smiled and said, 'That's exactly why we fix them up. We want them to get out there and live life.'"

I kissed Peggy on the cheek and held her close.

Church was our haven. We attended as a family, often carrying Matt and Sam in leg casts. We told the boys again and again how much Jesus loved them, that we all looked the same to him. As a child, I'd found my own salvation when I went to church and first heard those words, "Jesus loves you," from the Sunday school teacher. *Me? Jesus loves me?* I wondered if that could be true. But I was assured that, even though I was a scrappy, scrawny boy whose mother had left him in the dusty road, I was loved anyway. And that's what I told my sons. But would that be enough to prepare them for the often cruel world we lived in?

One year at Christmas, we had to rush Joshua to the hospital with an infection of the brain. At just ten years old and a mere thirty-five pounds, he'd had more than his share of surgeries, but this was his first time in the emergency room. The doctor's orders were for parents to wait in the hall. But Joshua started screaming, the kind of screaming that pierces your soul and doesn't stop. The kind where you want to run to his side to be with him, to do anything you can to lessen the pain. And they wouldn't let me in.

"Do you hear that screaming?" I said to the first doctor I saw. He started to walk past me, but I grabbed his collar. "That's my son! I want to be with him! I'll break down that door if you don't let me in." I meant it too. They could get as many guys in white coats as they could find to hold me down, but I'd fight them to be by my son's side.

The doctor spoke to a nurse, and she came over. "We'll give you a try."

I went in and put my arm around Joshua. "I'm here, Josh. Dad's here," I said calmly.

His screaming stopped, and the monitors settled into a more stable rhythm. Why couldn't they understand that he just needed some tender loving care?

Our sweet Ruth lived a life in and out of hospital waiting rooms. Between Matt, Josh, and Sam, there were a total of fifty-three surgeries through the years. One time, while Josh was in the hospital for an extended period, we felt Ruthie needed an escape. Matt and Sam were in leg casts again, so we put them in wheelchairs and the five of us headed out to walk across the Golden Gate Bridge. The San Francisco air smelled fresh, and the water glistened below the expanse of the towering steel cables that supported the bridge high in the air.

It was then that I felt the massive support of God. I realized that he had cradled me in his arms as a small boy lying in the dusty road and as a grown man when I cried out to him to help my sons find their way in the world. He had not abandoned me as a child, and he would not abandon my sons. I could feel the strength and courage God had given me. Like that bridge, I was supported. We returned to the hospital that day and faced another operation for Joshua. He survived that surgery and the others that followed over the next twenty-four years.

It was a heartbreaking blow when Josh passed away at the age of thirty-four, but for a boy who wasn't supposed to survive the day of his birth, Joshua put up a good fight. And I needn't have worried about my other sons finding jobs, falling in love, marrying, and having children. They were accomplishing all of those things.

Sam graduated with honors from the San Francisco Art Institute in 1993, and today he is an acclaimed artist. He married and has three children. Ruth became a nurse, married a doctor, and is the mother of twin girls.

Matt rose through the ranks in the business world, closing deals with some of Silicon Valley's most well-known companies. He is a former president of Little People of America, where he met his wife. Matt was twenty-six when he married Amy, also a little person. Together, they now own and operate Roloff Farms, a sprawling thirty-four-acre farm in Oregon. I'm a grandpa to their four children, one of whom has dwarfism as well.

In 2004, Matt came to me one day and said, "Dad, our family has been asked to do a television program. It will show people how normal our family really is. Maybe it can even bridge the gap between what people know and don't know about dwarfism."

I looked at Matt sitting across the table from me. His legs didn't reach the floor from the stool he sat on, and the crutches he used to get around were propped up next to the counter, but we were more alike than I had realized on the day he was born. He had the same stubborn streak and outspoken attitude that Peggy always said I had. And he was as protective and proud of his kids as I was of mine.

But whereas I had wanted to stop the stares, Matt had the courage to stand tall and say to the world, *Look at me, look at my family, look at who we really are. Yes, we look different. Yes, we have different abilities. But in our souls and in our lives, we're not so different from you.*

"I think the TV show is a great idea," I said to Matt.

God had given Peggy and me the courage and strength to raise our extraordinary children, and now it was Matt's turn. Though we are all different on the outside, on the inside we are very much alike, with hopes and dreams for a bright future. I never would have imagined, back when Peggy and I held our first son Matt in our arms, that life would turn out the way it has. We are truly blessed. And I am so proud of all of our children.

—*B. J. Taylor, as told by Ron Roloff*

A Place in the Class

On the form for Gabriela's education plan there's a space marked "Your Child's Future. Let us know what you think your child will be doing in two years, five years, ten years." I leave this space blank. I envy parents who plan their kid's future—a car, a college education, a wedding. My view is every seven to ten days, the cycle of Gabriela's grand mal seizures. I have rescheduled birthday parties, walked out of performances, and canceled vacations because of her seizures. They come unannounced and without cause or provocation.

Her eighth-grade year has been especially difficult, with trials of new seizure medications. Their harsh side effects cost her almost four months of school. So, when parents begin to plan the eighth-grade graduation ceremonies a year in advance, I don't volunteer. I pretend that it's not important to me, to Gabriela, or to anyone else.

During the school year, I read about graduation activities in every parent newsletter. Save the dates. Dress codes. Schedule of events. Timing. "If you are making a reservation for lunch after the graduation, make your reservations after 1:00 P.M."

A week before the graduation, my neighbor, Sally, who doesn't have a child in the class, informs me that she will be there. Sally has four children in and out of our town's school system. "Because we don't have a high school, middle-school graduation is a big deal here," Sally tells me one afternoon as we wait on the parking lot for the after-school pick-up. "Some children have been together since pre-K. When they go off to their different high schools, they may not see each other again. This is the big send-off."

Gabriela, her father Gary, and I moved here seven years ago. We fled from a small town in New England, where we were told that Gabriela was incapable of learning and that she should be placed in a program for the severely disabled. They assumed that because Gabriela couldn't speak she had nothing to say, that she didn't need to express her feelings. They thought that because she had seizures she had limited intelligence, that she had no ideas or opinions about books or movies or the people in her life. Three thousand miles away, we found a school that welcomed children with multiple challenges and a school district that supported Gabriela's inclusion in regular classes.

Gabriela's occupational therapist tells me she wants to come to graduation. Her aides from fourth and fifth grade and her speech pathologist from sixth grade say they might be there, too. They remind me that Gabriela will be the first graduate in the middle school's history who uses synthesized speech. I can no longer ignore this event. I hope they are not disappointed, but I tell myself that they all know Gabriela. Some days she's on; some days she's not.

Like most of us, Gabriela communicates in several different ways: facial expressions, body language, eye gaze, blinking for "yes" and a multiple-choice system that bears some resemblance to the game Twenty Questions. With this method, the communication partner (usually a teacher, an aide, or me) offers a set of three choices, followed by a choice of "something else." Gabriela answers each question until she is satisfied with the final response. Sometimes her answers are programmed into her communication device, a computer with synthesized speech, so she can speak in her own voice.

All of Gabriela's school assignments were tackled with this slow, painstaking process. Phrase by phrase, pausing after each choice to give her time to respond, I helped her compose essays, reports, and projects. It took practice. Over time, with the help of a few gifted teachers, I became more proficient at asking questions and reading Gabriela's responses. I wasn't always successful. Sometimes, I didn't present the right choices for Gabriela, especially on more complex subjects, like the significance of stars light years away or the relevance of a Robert Frost poem ("Is it nature, loss, fear of the unknown, or something else?"). There were many times when both of us would dissolve into separate pools of frustration. Then there were days when her seizures or her medications to control them caused her to lose focus, and she couldn't respond at all.

On graduation day, Gary and I follow directions and drop off Gabriela at the auditorium's back door one hour before the ceremony. Her aide, Lauren, greets us and rolls Gabriela to where the graduates are congregating. Gabriela smiles as she approaches the other kids. We stand waiting for her to look back, but she doesn't. At fourteen, she is happy to get away from us.

The auditorium is divided into two sections, blue and gold, the school's colors. All the other parents know their assignments. Gary and I don't know if we are blue or gold. I start to worry that there is something else that everyone else knows and we don't. We sit in the last row of the blue side, the side closest to the exit. I slouch down in my seat and check the time. Two more hours and this will all be over, plenty of time to conjure up worst-case scenarios. She won't be able to hold her head up. She'll fall asleep. The bright stage lights will blind her. She'll cough or choke and interrupt the ceremony. She'll have a seizure.

I watch the other parents file in. The more experienced know to save seats for friends and family. A few rows in front of us, Maggie Stone takes off her black silk jacket and carefully spreads the sleeves out across the backs of four seats. She nods and smiles at me. She usually ignores me. Some people don't know how to respond to Gabriela. She makes them uncomfortable. They know they shouldn't stare, but then what? So they wave their magic wands and—poof! She doesn't exist. Before I had Gabriela, I had a magic wand, too.

I sit up and look around for my few friends. They must all be sitting on the gold side. I worked hard to make friends here. Hot lunch committee. Community service. Room mother and driver on countless field trips. I volunteer for myself as much as for Gabriela, not just to get involved in the school community but also to observe what nondisabled children do, what they say, and what they think about. This was my education.

The auditorium starts to vibrate with excitement and anticipation. The hum hurts my ears. Parents are greeting each other—grinning, waving, shaking hands. Many are hugging and kissing. Their shared pride is palpable. Everyone is exuberant. Younger siblings, who can't wait in their seats, run up and down the aisles. Their giddiness makes me nervous.

I am consumed by apprehension for Gabriela. I worry that the sounds or the flashbulbs might agitate her. The school orchestra has been tuning their instruments for more than half an hour; the noise reverberates against the auditorium's walls. Only five more minutes and the ceremony will begin. I feel hot, then cold. I take off my jacket, carefully folding it on my lap. Then I put it back on again.

Finally, the orchestra begins to play "Pomp and Circumstance," and the students begin the processional down the aisles. Two at a time, alternating boys and girls, they appear at the doorway. Boys, dressed in dark sport coats and ties, dangle their arms at their sides, not comfortable in their clothes or their bodies. Girls, in white dresses, appear in every stage of development, from short, thin little slips of girls to tall, full-bosomed young women with waists and hips. Most chose slinky spaghetti strap dresses that reveal their forms. They hold yellow roses and try to balance in their high heels. I remember some of these girls from the elementary school Girl Scout troop—the shy ones who worked quietly on woven placemats and the boisterous ones who cracked jokes and disrupted our meetings. The shy ones often befriended Gabriela . . . until the seventh grade, when they all discovered boys. The girls skipped lunch and waited for boys by the side of the cafeteria. And Gabriela was left behind to eat with her aide, Lauren.

The pace of the processional is painfully slow. I can't discern the order. It's not alphabetical. Is it by home room? I start to panic. I can't find my child. Maybe she had a seizure and was pulled from the line. As the first students take their places on stage, I realize the order is by height. Gabriela will be near the end, with the shortest. She holds up her head as Lauren rolls her down the aisle, the rose placed in the middle of her tray table. The other children march up the steps to the stage. Then I notice that the stage isn't ramped. What will happen to Gabriela at the foot of the stairs? Surely, they're not planning to lift her in her chair. I lose sight of her near the bottom of the aisle. I lean over and whisper to Gary, "Where's Gabriela?"

"Take it easy. She's in good hands," he whispers back.

At last, she reappears. Lauren has rolled her out the exit and re-entered by way of a backstage door. They take their places with the class. One hundred forty children perch on ten rows of risers, fourteen to a row, the tallest at the top.

My eyes fix on Gabriela. She is in the front row. With her ever-present tremor, her left hand rhythmically taps her tray table. Lauren wipes the saliva from the corner of her mouth with a cotton handkerchief.

The school superintendent speaks first. Then a member of the school board begins, "I just have a few words . . ." But her speech seems endless.

Gabriela continues to face forward. Is she looking for us? Even if we'd sat in the front row, her vision is too poor to see us. I tell myself that she knows we are out there watching her. We have told her over and over, "We're very proud of you."

The principal addresses the audience. "Please hold your applause until the end of each row." The first row stands, and the principal calls each student's name. The children know exactly what to do, and each follows the rhythm like a well-rehearsed, albeit stiff and awkward, dance. One by one they walk to center stage. A name is called. The student turns to face the audience, walks to the side to shake hands with the principal, and receives the scrolled paper.

"Jennifer Wheeler."

"Go Jenny," a single voice from the audience yells out.

"James Campbell."

"Anne Newton."

There are a few cat calls, no doubt from older siblings, but this is a rule-abiding group. Most people follow instructions and sit motionless after each name.

"Thomas Lee."

"Gabriela Cellini."

Applause starts softly, then rolls across the seats and fills the hall. Gabriela is not the last in the row. Gary and I turn to each other. We mirror each other's expression of amazement.

They're actually applauding for Gabriela. I'm not sure why she gets this special recognition, but as I look around, it seems to be shared.

Tears blur my sight of Gabriela, who is now center stage, her blonde curls glowing from the stage lights. Exuberant, she grins back at the audience. Her aide pushes her chair over to the principal, who touches Gabriela's hand and places the diploma on her tray table. Gabriela looks up in acknowledgment and goes back to her place with the class.

—Harriet Heydemann Cellini

Are You Done Feeling Sorry for Yourself?

On a cold December morning in 1991, I was sitting in the pediatric intensive care unit staring out at the street below. The cold rain that washed down the outside of the windows seemed to reflect the bleakness inside my soul as I pondered the last few months. Four weeks earlier, my youngest daughter Allie had been born with Down syndrome and severe heart defects. She had faced one emergency after another in her very short lifespan, and it seemed as if we had been living on a roller coaster. I longed for our worn brown sofa at home and the flickering flames of our fireplace, instead of this sterile hospital room with its monitors and machines.

This was Allie's third hospitalization, and it seemed as if we knew the ICU staff better than our own friends and family. During Allie's hospital stays, I seldom left her bedside. I was able to breastfeed her every couple of hours, and I knew that every precious ounce of milk carried vital antibodies and nourishment to her frail body. Now it looked as though we would spend Christmas and New Year's Eve in the hospital, and the very thought was unbearable. I stared out at the gloomy weather and felt my spirits plummet even further.

Glancing at a mirror on the far wall, I could see a reflection of myself as I sat in a worn burgundy lounge chair next to Allie's cold metal crib. This impersonal hospital room is certainly not the place I had envisioned for mother-daughter bonding. I had carefully scooped up my daughter along with her dangling tubes and monitor lines and had propped her against my upraised knees. Her blue eyes gazed contentedly into mine and her little fists rested quietly at her side.

Doctors and nurses popped in and out of the room, always bringing some version of bad news. "Time to draw more blood." "She's not gaining any weight—she really needs to nurse more." "We need to insert another line into her veins for more medicine." Just that morning, we had been told that her immune system was poorly developed and that she had virtually no protection against the cold and flu-causing viruses that were rampant in our community that winter.

Originally due in December, Allie had been born several weeks early. Because of her heart problems, the delivery was high-risk and there were perhaps a dozen people milling around in the labor room. After her tiny head emerged from the birth canal, the obstetrician gently rotated her face toward me. I will always remember my first view of her still-moist face, with the characteristic features of trisomy 21 clearly etched in her lovely features. While no tests had prepared me for the possibility, I certainly was at the age when genetic disorders are more common. *My beautiful, long-awaited daughter has Down syndrome,* I remember thinking very clearly, even before her lower body emerged from my womb.

At the time of Allie's birth, I believed I was prepared for the mental retardation and physical differences that accompanied her disability. I had grown up with a close friend who had Down syndrome and thought I knew what to expect. However, I found myself totally devastated by Allie's severe heart problems and breathing difficulties. She had a huge hole in the center of her heart, and all four chambers were connected in a bizarre configuration that was robbing her body of the oxygen it needed to survive. Even with heavy doses of heart medicines, her little body seemed to be losing its will to survive.

I had been doing a great deal of reading about Down syndrome since Allie's birth and assumed that she would face incredible obstacles in her lifetime. As I sat in the hospital holding my infant daughter, for some reason, my thoughts lingered on the special occasions she might miss—the high school prom, dating, a loving husband, childbirth, the joys of motherhood, the challenges of a high-powered career. Tears flowed down my face as I stared blindly at the wall, absorbed in my grief.

Suddenly, I looked up and noticed a curly-haired woman in a white lab coat standing at the foot of the crib. She smiled warmly and spoke softly, "Hello, I'm Carole. You must be Allison's mother. I'm a pediatric cardiology nurse. I work with Allison's doctors and wondered if you might have a moment to talk to me."

"Sure, sit down," I murmured uncomfortably. While part of me was glad to have company during the long day, I also felt a surge of resentment that my private grief was visible to a stranger. But then, our lives had lost all semblance of privacy and normalcy since Allie's birth.

"How are things going for the two of you?" Carole inquired.

"How are things going? What do you think? They're awful, terrible, unbearable—I don't know what else to say!" The words tumbled out of my mouth in unstoppable streams: worries about Allie's survival, the misery of sitting for endless days and nights in the chaotic intensive care unit, and the terrible thoughts I had been pondering about Allie's future.

Carole listened compassionately, nodding from time to time and saying little.

"This is all too much. I'm not ready for it. I just don't know if I can do it,"

Finally, I wound down and stared mutely at her.

Carole sat thoughtfully for a moment before responding, "It really must seem quite overwhelming to you right now. It's not at all what you expected, is it?"

"No, it's not. She's adorable, she's ours, and we love her dearly. But I just don't know how to handle all the problems she's going to face. Will she have friends in school, or will she be teased and bullied? Who will take her to the prom? Will she have babies, will I be a grandmother? Will she be able to drive a car? But most of all, will she even survive the holidays? She's so very sick right now. Just look at her!"

Carole nodded in understanding, "Yes, she is quite ill right now. Her heart isn't doing a very good job for the rest of her body, and we're going to have to repair it so she can survive and grow. That's real, that's immediate, and we do need to deal with it right away."

"This is too much, just too much. I don't know what to do." I sobbed in anger, "No one ever told me it would be like this."

Carole listened patiently for several more minutes until my words tapered off. She smiled gently at me and then said, "Okay. You have some very real issues and you have every right to complain. Now, are you ready to stop feeling sorry for yourself?"

I stared at her in disbelief. Had the woman even listened to a single word I'd been saying? How dare she! I had every right to be angry, and I deserved some sympathy for what had happened to our family! I wanted to scream and send her from the room, but something stopped me. I stared at her for long moments, while she gazed steadily into my eyes. Finally, I choked out, "What in the world do you mean by that?"

"You have every right to be upset. Your baby is critically ill, you're worried about her future, and you're sick and tired of this hospital and everyone in it. You've been at your daughter's bedside most of the past month, and you're just plain worn down," she stated evenly.

"So what did you mean when you said I was feeling sorry for myself?" I replied.

"I simply believe that your life would be much more bearable if you could learn to look at events through Allison's eyes instead of your own. Look at her—she's perfectly happy and content with life. She shares none of your worries. She feels your love, she tastes your warm breast milk, and she hears your loving voice talking to her. For Allison, life is full of joy and peace."

I stared at Carole in disbelief, wounded by her insensitive and callous words. Incredulous, I waited for her to take them back and apologize. Long minutes went by as we looked intently at one another. I was the first to break eye contact, clutching Allie protectively to my bosom. I turned away to stare out the window once more before looking down at my precious daughter. She opened her lovely blue eyes briefly to gaze at me and then closed them again in contentment. Carole was right—all was well in Allie's small world.

With trembling hands, I reached out to grasp Carole's hand. I was momentarily taken aback when I noticed the tears in her eyes. Indeed, life would have its share of troubles and setbacks for my beloved little daughter. But always, I would be better off looking at life through Allie's eyes. Her eyes see only love and happiness, her heart knows only joy and love, and her arms know only hugs and friendship.

It's been sixteen years since that cold December day in the intensive care unit. Allie has had several open-heart surgeries. She still has limitations to her endurance and strength and uses a wheelchair for long excursions. But life, through Allie's eyes, is magnificent. There are no strangers, only valued friends. Many times, I've thought back to the message that Carole shared with us. As harsh as her words sounded at the time, I realize that she said exactly what I needed to know at the precise moment that my heart was ready to listen.

And yes, there are still days when I feel sorry for myself, or worse, when I go so far as to pity Allie. When other children at the park rebuff Allie, when she can't play soccer in the recreation league because of her disabilities, or when she is the last one chosen for a game—that hurts. There's no way to pretend that it doesn't. At times like those, I take a deep breath and search for those quiet words in my heart, "Look at life through Allison's eyes." To Allie, there is always another playmate when one shies away from my daughter's differences. Although soccer remains an unattainable goal, Allie has become a proficient horsewoman in our local therapeutic horseback riding program, a special needs cheerleader with a smile a mile wide, and a Special Olympics swim team champion.

What's more, my own life is richer and finer by far because I am Allie's mother. If she hadn't been born, if she hadn't persevered through adversity, I would never have known her angelic spirit. And I would never have known the unadulterated joy of looking at life through Allie's eyes.

—*Sandy Keefe*

Le Mot Juste

"Don't let her water board," my sister warned. "She just had her rotator cuff operated on. So water boarding is out of the question."

I assured her that I would not let my niece torture anyone while on a visit to the lake.

My sister grew quiet, then chuckled. "I meant wake board."

My family has a genetic disposition for malapropisms. When my geezer dad asks for the zipper while stationed in front of the TV, I give him the remote control. The etymology of "zipper" is this: He's thinking of the word "zapper" and gets it confused with "zipper." For him, the microwave is the "radar range" and a "calculator" is a "computer." In Dad-speak, I feel I am deciphering tricky crossword puzzles with off-the-wall clues.

My father's father used to whistle when he got stuck on a word. Then, he'd snap his fingers and flap his hands; someone would supply the word for him by the end of his routine. I think my father-in-law had the most effective method, though. He called everything "thing-a-ma-jig."

My kids also confuse words constantly. Grammar too. Although the product of an elite college education, my one son insists on beginning every sentence with "Me." "Me an'" starts most discourse. "Me an' Ben are going swimming," he remarks.

"I don't think Ben is mean," is my reply.

When my son can't find a word, he doesn't whistle; he uses the words "like" or "you know." His speech goes this way: "You know, like, me and Ben, like are, you know goin', like, swimmin'."

I try to use the *mot juste*. When my grown kids say, "Pass me, like, the vinegar and oil doohickey," I respond, "Cruet?"

"Whatever," they say.

They call bacon bits "meaties" and spaghetti "ghetti." The individual sharp points of the fork to them are "prongs." I correct them: "Tines?"

"Whatever." They shrug me off.

Yet, my kids seem to have mastered all the computer jargon and speak-ease of e-mail and text messaging. I read their missives that are a series of alphabet soup, such as "lol," "btw," "cya," and "ttyl." All the icons they recognize and know their meanings. Most are Greek to me.

I guess *le mot juste* depends on one's generation as much as on one's education or one's handicaps. As with everything else in the world, only change is constant. *Le mot juste* for our offspring will be technology inspired. And old boomers like me will soon reply "whatever" to our grandkids as they correct our antiquated vocabulary.

Of course, sometimes finding the right word is a more serious problem and does signify a learning disability. One of my sons stuttered badly, refused to read, couldn't stay on task, and did poorly in first grade. They tested him. Attention deficit disorder without hyperactivity was the verdict. Speech therapy was recommended, too. Yet, he still didn't thrive.

When schooling woes continued into middle school, we took him to the university for more tests. They decided he had "severe auditory processing problems." His school made academic adjustments as well as learning-disability accommodations for him, such as placing him close to the front of the class, tapping on his desk to bring his attention back to task, repeating more slowly the homework assignments, and writing assignments on the board as well.

Still, he had trouble with social nuances and with appropriate behavior in social situations. A psychologist thought we should take him to be tested for autism.

I drove him to the University of North Carolina's TEACCH clinic, (Treatment and Education of Autistic and related Communication-handicapped CHildren). They said he had some of the symptoms of Asperger's disorder but not enough to qualify him as such.

On the way home, I explained the diagnosis to my preteen son.

Shaking his head, he turned to me and said, "Mom, you could have saved a lot of time and money."

"How's that?" I asked.

"I could have told you I am no ass bugger."

The years have passed. Schooling was always a challenge, peer interaction an even larger problem. My son did go to college and graduated. He still makes poor choices and still has questionable judgment in choosing appropriate friends, but he has also developed some admirable qualities, perhaps as a direct result of his struggles and weakness. He has compassion—especially for old folks, little kids, and all animals. He is generous with his time and resources and is a friend to those in need. He has learned to banter, joke, keep it light, and control his temper so that he doesn't find himself on the other side of a flung fist.

My message to parents of children with special needs is an old one: This, too, shall pass. Stages come and go, and needs change. You can't predict the future or change the past. So don't worry over either. Things work out. Love your kid. Help him or her and appreciate what you have. As the French say, "In the kingdom of the blind, the one-eyed man is king." Be grateful for the assets your child possesses, compliment his successes, and minimize his failures. After all, he without fault can throw the first stone; we are all imperfect, limited, and challenged in one way or another. *Le mot juste*—the right word—is always "accept!"

—*Erika Hoffman*

Lighting the Way

The gymnasium is packed with families seated around a dozen banquet tables. Decorated Christmas trees stud the corners of the room, and red and green crepe paper streamers ribbon the walls. A banner stretched across the stage at the front of the room reads: "Happy Holidays from Uptown Downs!"

This is the first time my children and I have come to the annual holiday breakfast hosted by our local Down syndrome support group. The room is crowded and hot and noisy with the din of hundreds of people. The tables are full of plates of pancakes and sausage and cups of orange juice, some of which have been knocked over by kids' elbows. My toddler Thomas is squirming on my lap, and my older kids are arguing over who has the most syrup. I'd been looking forward to this event for weeks, but now I'm beginning to wish we'd just stayed home.

Then the lights dim, and the dancers take the stage.

Wearing red sequined jackets and black pants, a dozen children and teenagers with Down syndrome line up in position. "Please welcome the Sparkly Pals," announces the emcee. As a heavy funk beat begins, the dancers set in motion with a hip-hop routine. In unison, they twist and twirl, bounce and bend.

"You'd better get this party started," the lyrics ring out.

And we do. Within moments, the hundreds of people in the audience are clapping in time with the music, cheering aloud as the dancers strut their stuff.

I clap along with the crowd, amazed that I feel so comfortable. The year before, soon after Thomas was born with Down syndrome, I saw the holiday breakfast advertised on the Uptown Downs' website and wondered if I'd ever want to attend. I couldn't imagine walking into a party full of kids with Down syndrome and their families.

Actually, I could imagine, and the image made me squirm. I pictured myself standing awkwardly in a corner, holding Thomas, unsure of how to interact. The people with Down syndrome I'd met in the past made me uneasy. Thoughts, feelings, quirks, whims—everything about them was right up front, right on the surface. Their lack of self-consciousness increased my own. I didn't know how to respond to such spontaneity and openness.

Funny—that same openness seems delightful now. These red-sequined dancers have no inhibitions. They move with utter freedom, with the joy and confidence of being at ease in their own skins. And that ease is rubbing off on the rest of us. My kids grin at me and point to their favorite dancers onstage. On my lap, Thomas rocks to the beat. In a few years he'll be old enough to join the dance troupe. I can't wait.

After the hip-hop number comes a holiday medley. During "Santa Claus Is Coming to Town," a teen boy in a leather jacket and a red Santa hat takes center stage and strikes Elvis-style poses, while a posse of teen girls dances around him. A gorgeous little girl with long brown hair and tiny glasses dances solo to "I Saw Mommy Kissing Santa Claus." The final number, "Jingle Bell Rock," brings down the house. Flushed and happy, we cheer wildly as the dancers bow.

The crowd quiets as the next group of performers comes onstage: madrigal singers from the local high school. Sixteen in all, the girls wear matching emerald-green formal dresses, the boys wear tuxedoes. They sing with measured voices polished to a shine, moving gracefully into different formations with slick theatrical style. Chestnuts roast in the warm glow of their voices; sleigh bells ring in pitch-perfect harmony.

The piano accompaniment ends, and the madrigals begin singing a cappella, a beautiful Christmas song I've never heard before. Round, clear notes soar through the room, creating a magical moment when the world stills and the air fills with beauty.

But instead of joy, my heart wells up with incredible sadness. These young men and women are breathtakingly talented, bright and beautiful as snowflakes, brimming over with gifts for the world. The contrast between them and the Sparkly Pals twists my heart with grief.

Then a new song starts. "Rudolph the red-nosed reindeer . . ."

The kids in the audience—those with Down syndrome and those without—sing along with the madrigals, shouting "like a lightbulb!" and "like Monopoly!" at the right times. But I can't smile. Thomas will never be able to compete with these super kids onstage and the "normal" kids in the audience. He'll struggle to learn basic skills that they pick up without effort, and even if he does his very best, he still won't measure up. I picture people staring at Thomas, teasing him, ridiculing him. He doesn't have a shiny red nose, but because of his extra chromosome he'll forever stick out in a crowd, just like Rudolph.

Smiling as they sing, the girls in formal dresses stretch their arms forward, beckoning for the kids with Down syndrome in the front rows to join them onstage. Then the guys motion with their arms, inviting those in the back rows to come forward. Adults hoist the children up one by one until the stage is full.

They sing together onstage, arms around each other's shoulders, swaying to the music in an unlikely combination of formal gowns, tee-shirts, tuxedos, and bright red sequined jackets. The madrigals' careful steps give way to easy, spontaneous movement. Bow ties are knocked askew. Tendrils of hair escape from the girls' elegant up-dos. Within moments, they've transformed from meticulous performers to starry-eyed children eager for Christmas.

By the time "Rudolph" ends and "Jingle Bells" begins, my sadness is gone. Kids with Down syndrome might not ever look or sound like madrigal singers, but they have other gifts to give the world. I see those gifts onstage now in vibrant color. Friendship flows with the music, and pure joy shines on every face. I realize that every person, no matter how many chromosomes they have, can offer peace on earth and goodwill toward men—the ultimate gift. And we might be surprised by who ends up lighting the way.

—Kathryn Lynard Soper

A Vertical Victory

For a vertically challenged family like ours, the ski slopes are a foreign land. Long before our daughter was diagnosed with cerebral palsy, we committed ourselves to the pool and accessible ground.

So, when the invitation comes for us to participate in a ski program in Colorado, I am skeptical. But after some research and reading, my curiosity gets the better of me. Before I can stop myself, I've agreed to bring Gemma along for the ride.

March midterm break is a fine excuse for adventure. I sign up a friend with the strength to help lift Gemma, pack the car to its hilt, and kiss my husband goodbye. We leave the city in a darkening twilight. With the temperature at minus twenty-five and dropping, the cold is bitter. It feels good to leave Winnipeg winter behind.

At the border, our tight packing pays off unexpectedly. As one of the unlucky two percent, we are pulled over for a long search and potential seizure by U.S. Customs. When the customs officer realizes the depth of our luggage and my despair at her request, she experiences an abrupt change of heart and waves us away. We breathe a sigh of relief and start to laugh. We are on our way!

Two long days of driving into the night and 1,017 miles bring us to Denver. The geese have begun to fly, but now so has the snow and it is becoming dark. As we leave the city, fog compounds the darkness. Lights racing past us are a blur of white and yellow flashes. I can't see the front of the car. Motorists on either side of me, no doubt familiar to the highway, travel at alarming speed. My stomach is clutched so tightly that I can't press the gas pedal any farther. I can hear my heart beating; I can hear my breath inhaling and exhaling. I can hardly hear Lori and Gemma in the back seat. We've already gotten lost leaving the city. Now it is up to me to find the right exit from this twenty-first–century nightmare.

If I had a moment to contemplate, I might recall that my very first freeway experience was in Denver, thirty years earlier. With three girlfriends, I had driven south in a rented car. We'd been lost then, too, and I'd been alarmed by the feel of all those cars on the highway with me. Back then, it was midsummer. Back then, it seemed that, as soon as I'd caught up with their speed, a traffic light demanded an immediate stop. Now, though, I have no time to reflect on the past. Speed defines the moment. Perhaps I'll encounter traffic lights. Miraculously, we find the exit.

Still blinded by the blizzard, I skid to a stop, unsure whether the animal in front of us is a mountain goat or a deer. The mountain itself sheers upward on our right, inches from my right fender. I will my pulse to slow down and resume the drive.

We careen up and down the mountains in the fog, caught up by a force stronger than ourselves, thrusting us forward. When the fog lifts, my headlights catch sight of signs warning us of "Falling Rock." We laugh hysterically, our mirth edged with terror. The sign saying "Avalanche Blasting" sets us off into gales of giggles. To three prairie ladies driving blind up mountainsides, each sign seems funnier than the last. Our pent-up nervous energy topples over, unchecked. I beg Lori to share a smoke. As the mountains press in on us, she embodies my unspoken fear, despite her encouragement. A cigarette might release us. We work wordlessly together to keep Gemma calm. No twelve-year-old should have to know the extent of our anxieties.

When the fog lifts, my spirits lift a little, as well, but it is too dark to relax and the snow is falling fast. Thank goodness prairie driving has made me tough. I've survived blizzards and black ice, and I know how to gear down without braking to make the turns. Here, there are no straight stretches to lull me to sleep. We twist upward and dash down again, never daring to stop. If we stop, surely somebody will bump us! We marvel at the way drivers speed past us. Slowing down behind a wheezing Winnebago, we wonder, "Why don't they pull over?" Their bed is attached. Ours, ahead and reserved with plastic, has yet to be achieved. The toxic air of the Winnebago creeps inside our car and makes us all nauseous. I have to pass, and manage.

The road continues. A sign announces it is only twenty-four miles to Winter Park, but it takes us hours. Steep downward curves follow corkscrew turns upward; then suddenly the sign warns "Steep Hill." How much more extreme can it be? A Safeway transport truck speeds past, just as I am wondering how the large transport trucks maneuver these roads. We are wound as tightly as corkscrews, and the final lag becomes endless. Five miles seem like fifty. Will we ever get there? I begin to flag. Then Gemma senses the change and starts to whine.

"One more curve; one more mountain peak," I assure her, praying I am right.

I've never liked roller coasters, and this drive feels like the feared fair ride—one that I can't get off. Pushing toward speed and oblivion is not my style. So what am I doing, taking us all onto the ski slopes? Am I nuts?

When a perky night clerk welcomes us at the end of the trip, I growl, "That mountain ride was the worst of my life."

We need food, and the only restaurant is about to close. Never has a smoke-filled pub looked so good nor a congealed cheddar cheese soup tasted so acceptable.

Next day, the sun stumbles over the mountaintop. Our floor-to-ceiling window looks onto a postcard view with its evergreens and its rocky floor dusted with snow and drifts. Last night's nightmare begins to recede. Now, skiing assumes an imminent reality. Gemma can't walk. How will she ski?

Everyone who gets off the elevator, looking healthy and tired, seems able-bodied. Have I made a mistake?

At last, we check into Winter Park's National Sports Center for the Disabled, tucked into a corner of the buildings at the base of the mountain. The day is sunny and damp. Snow is falling—or does it fall off mountains like it falls off prairie trees, making it appear to be a snowfall?

At the center, disability is the norm. An in-your-face nonchalance directs all interactions. "I don't dream of walking anymore. That's too SLOW," reads one poster, showing a one-legged skier on the slopes.

In the equipment room, we're greeted by a man whose moustache arches over his smile. Talking first to Gemma to ease her shyness, he outfits her with goggles and beautiful ski mitts plus two wonderful volunteers. Jana and Lee reassure me that Gemma will be fine. Jana's ease at communicating with my nonverbal daughter puts me at ease and I feel my smile return to my face.

It takes hours for people of every shape and disability to wheel in and get outfitted to ski, and Gemma grows impatient. Finally, Gemma is taken out to the mountain; Lori and I follow.

The volunteers decant Gemma from her chair onto a curious contraption: a sit-ski, like a high-tech sled with two hourglass-shaped skis attached to the bottom. After wrapping various bungee cords around her, they pronounce Gemma ready to go, and she joins an enormous lineup at the lift.

It is the closest I've ever been to a ski hill, and if I weren't plagued with doubts about the sanity of this situation, I would probably be nonplussed by all those fit figures, complete with skis, goggles, and colorful attire, all politely lining up to ride to the top of the mountain. But I'm too curious to feel out of place.

Despite the length of the queue, Gemma and her two volunteers are quickly admitted to the head of the lineup, with smiles and courtesy. The lift doesn't stop; it merely slows down slightly while two able-bodied volunteers lift Gemma and her sit-ski onto the lift and then hop aboard with their own skis attached to their feet. I'm already in awe of them.

But then the fear and waiting begins. I watch the lift ascend the mountain until I can no longer see the upward-bound trio. I struggle to find myself a proper vantage point. Behind us, I overhear that for the past two years, the program, with about a thousand volunteers, has suffered shortages of volunteers because lift prices have dropped, making it less desirable to trade assistance for free lifts. Volunteers need advanced skiing abilities to act as instructors to people like my triplegic daughter, whose attitude remains one of smiles and excitement. They also need strength; the volunteers' stories about back aches and cures exchanged are legion. The six days of training and the ten days of teaching in a single ski season (mid-November to mid-April) is a significant commitment. I learn that most of the volunteers come from Denver and manage that hair-raising drive regularly. Others come from the Fraser Valley, locally, and some from as far away as California, Minnesota, the East Coast, and Guam.

While I'm still waiting for Gemma to appear in my view, a bevy of English men in chairs arrive ready to hit the slopes. "If you can get to our office, then we can get you up on the slopes," the Winter Park NSCD literature boasts. Who am I to argue? In Europe, other skiers are disdainful of their disabled compatriots, but Americans have gone way past that attitude. At Winter Park, I see the skiers take others of all shapes in stride as long as they can manage the slopes. Matt Feeney, an extreme athlete of incredible skills and daring, in a chair since a diving accident, and a number of others continue to set the pace.

My bottom is beginning to feel the hard chair. Lori and I say nothing to each other; both of us have our eyes trained toward the slopes. I watch as others descend in comparable sit-skis. Someone tells me that the old ones looked like bath tubs. I'm trying to cram knowledge and facts into my head to push out those recurrent fears of falling and images from movies, including some spectacular tumbles that disabled the able-bodied skiers themselves. I expect sirens, stretchers, and helicopters. Instead, I hear laughter and see competence and extreme skill. One man without legs bends his arms, leans his torso forward, and whizzes down the slopes on a mono-ski, alone.

Well, Gemma has volunteers, I tell myself. Though I'm unable to imagine how they're going to manage this, I wait expectantly.

I hold my breath as Gemma's familiar silver jacket comes into sight. She's positioned well in the sit-ski, and now I can imagine her beaming with delight. Behind her, Lee holds onto a harness that he slackens to allow her to control her own turns with her shoulders.

Will she tip over? Will she tumble down the mountainside and set off an avalanche of fellow skiers? I wonder. *Well, at least it won't disable her.*

They've told me she must learn how far out to lean without tipping. That's what skiing is all about, they said: learning how to stay up and to turn without tipping.

I'm watching as Gemma begins the descent, and I'm holding my breath. I can hear my heart beat. The sounds of the cafeteria have stilled to a dull roar. Then, as she gathers speed and whooshes downward toward me, I hear the sound of hysterical laughter. It's me, and I'm breathing. It's Gemma, and she's skiing. Wow!

—*Sarah Yates*

Reform School

On Katy's first day of school, I shoved my car door open against a fierce blustery wind, hoisted my fourteen-month-old daughter onto my hip, and tromped into our county developmental center.

"Hope this helps," I grumbled under my breath. "You're too heavy for me to carry anymore."

Inside, I scanned the classroom. Several other babies were already sitting on the floor or on tiny chairs. One child had Down syndrome. Another wore leg braces. The hands of a little boy curved backward; his eyes wandered. These would be my daughter's classmates.

As I entrusted Katy (and a clean disposable diaper) into her teacher's outstretched arms, I felt pierced by an arrow of doubt. *Babies still in diapers shouldn't have to go to school,* I thought. Once Katy understood that I was going to leave her there, she pushed away from her teacher, stretched one little arm toward me, and wailed. I left before I cried too.

Outside, I crossed the street to the park. Ignoring the wind, I sat on a swing and watched two squirrels chase each other as my thoughts drifted back to the path that had led to this day.

Since birth, Katy had not developed at the normal rate. For a while, I had excused her slow development as individual variation. Then I attributed it to her poor vision, sensitivity to light, and her bouncy, crossed eyes. Finally, I couldn't avoid the obvious and admitted to myself that something was very wrong. Just before her first birthday, I took Katy to her doctor for a checkup.

"I'm worried," I said. "I think she's way behind."

Katy liked our pediatrician, Dr. Frasier, a slender, peaceful man with thinning hair.

He set a camel-shaped animal cracker on the table and watched as Katy groped for it.

Nodding, he said, "I see what you mean. By now she should be using her thumb and fingers, not her whole hand."

I sighed.

"Put her down. Let's see how well she sits."

Filled with anxiety, I sat Katy on the floor and watched helplessly as she began to topple like a slow-falling bowling pin.

The doctor frowned. "She's delayed in both gross and fine motor skills, all right. But I don't think we can blame her low vision alone. I suggest testing."

It took three months to arrange an evaluation with the developmental center. When the day finally came, I sat in the assessment room and, with my heart in my throat and my stomach wrenching, I watched as my daughter failed one test assignment after another.

How did I let this happen? I scolded myself. Reason told me I didn't cause these problems. Yet, I felt somehow responsible.

The howling wind interrupted my thoughts. Sitting outside had become too uncomfortable, so I left the park and sat in my car, where I pulled out a book to read. But I couldn't focus. Instead, I recalled a phone conversation I'd had with the director of the developmental center about five days after that preliminary evaluation.

"Katy tested below normal and qualifies for our program!" she had said brightly, as if it was a great treat for me to hear my baby was developmentally delayed. "She can start on Monday. You'll get the official score in about a month, once we can test her more thoroughly. And don't worry; her attendance here at the center will make a big difference."

I reclined the driver's seat of my car and closed my eyes. One way or another, I'd soon discover whether she was right. Hopefully, this would be Katy's "reform" school.

A month later, Katy's full evaluation was complete. I attended a meeting where the center personnel discussed results and together we'd create an individual education plan (IEP).

When Katy's teacher, Mrs. Thompson, told me, "Your daughter enjoys class and gets along with the other children," I felt wary. Her kind, well-chosen words sounded more like a prelude to bad news than reassurance. "And we'll do another IEP at the end of the school year to report her progress."

"But what's her score? How did she do on the test?" I asked.

Mrs. Thompson slid some papers toward me. "I want to remind you that there's more to a child than just IQ."

Now, I was really worried.

She pointed to a graph that displayed several different areas of development with dots showing where my daughter scored compared to the average.

"As you can see, your daughter scored below normal in every area. We'll be working on her gross and fine motor skills as well as on her mental development to bring up those scores. Overall, her IQ tested at fifty-five."

I swallowed my distress. "That's half of normal!" I cried.

Mrs. Thompson must have recognized my alarm. Her face read like a sympathy card. "Many parents feel responsible for their child's low scores. But it's not your fault. And school will help her."

My head pounded; my chest felt tight. I rubbed my temples. "Thanks," I said.

But I didn't feel thankful. I felt sad and guilty. Of course, this was my fault. Didn't I give birth to this child? Didn't I wait almost a year to do something about it? Perhaps I didn't stimulate her the way she needed. Perhaps I failed in some other way. What would people think of me? I left with a heavy heart.

A few days later, on Sunday, I sat in church, unable to focus on the service. My mind kept drifting to school and tests and IQ. Then I noticed the baby in front of us. She was about a year old, a few months younger than Katy. When she tried to grab her mother's earring, the woman smiled, turned her ear away, and moved the baby off her lap. The child giggled and sat upright. *She can sit alone!* I marveled. Then the little girl looked at the choir across the church and clapped. *She can see all the way across the church!* I watched her turn, grab the back of the pew, and pull herself up to stand. *Wow, she can even stand!* As that baby bounced to the music, she flirted with the man next to me. He smiled and waved back. The baby reached for him.

I watched that child perform typical twelve-month-old baby activities, and I loved and hated her for doing so. The contrast slapped me: More than likely, Katy would never grab my earrings. She probably wouldn't even see them from my lap. She certainly couldn't see the choir members across the church. Would she ever sit or stand or walk on her own? *I don't know,* I thought. In that instant, jealousy ripped my soul and despair flooded in. Everything I expected and counted on—Katy's freedom, mobility, learning, life choices, along with my expectation for a predictable life—capsized. The enormity of my loss threatened to drown me in sorrow and despair.

"Take the baby," I whispered to my husband.

"What's wrong?" he asked.

I shook my head, darted from the pew, and hustled into the ladies room. There, I raced into a stall, locked the door, and slumped against the wall. Wave after wave of pain washed over me. Suddenly I understood that our daughter and the rest of our family would suffer in countless ways and countless times because she was different and had special needs, because others wouldn't understand, and because we loved her. Tears streamed down my cheeks, and I couldn't control my sobbing.

Perhaps I experienced the grief that every parent encounters when he or she realizes a child is imperfect and can't be fixed. But with most parents, that realization comes slowly with little events. During tee-ball practice Dad learns his son isn't athletic, for instance. Or the teacher tells Mom that Joey is a slow reader. For me, grief and loss condensed into one terrible, defining moment when my dreams of a "normal" child died. It was so painful I thought I would die, too.

I bawled for several minutes. Then, empty of tears and emotionally spent, I washed my puffy, red face and rejoined my family.

Several weeks later, when I arrived at school to pick up my daughter at the end of class one afternoon, Mrs. Thompson rushed toward me, grinning.

"Something marvelous happened. Come see!"

I followed her to another room. There, the physical therapist said, "Katy, go to your mommy."

My daughter stood. Then she took one hesitant step . . . and another. After three more tiny steps, she plopped down and a wide, crazy grin spread across her face. At eighteen months of age, when most toddlers are running and perhaps even skipping, Katy finally walked!

I once heard someone say that having a child born with special needs is like stepping off a plane expecting to arrive in Cancun, Mexico, but discovering you've landed in Beijing, China, instead. You don't understand the language or culture, and you don't have the correct attire for the place. It's so different from what you expected, you feel completely disoriented and depressed. But eventually, as you learn the language and understand the culture, you embrace that foreign land as your own.

That's how it was. It took me eighteen months to accept Katy for who she was: a beautiful, loving child who just happened to have poor vision, an uncoordinated body, and slow development. I couldn't measure or judge her by the "normal" yardstick. Katy was unique, and her accomplishments would occur in their own way and at her own pace. As important, I finally understood that I wasn't responsible for my daughter's problems. Instead, I was responsible for helping her grow through them.

When I thought about it, I realized that the developmental center wasn't only reforming my daughter, it was also reforming me.

I gave Katy a hug. If she had been graduating from college, I wouldn't have been more proud.

—Ellen Tomaszewski

Oh, the Perilous Paddleboats

It is a warm summer day on Cape Cod. My five-year-old son Nicholas and I wait in line for the paddleboats. My husband Pete, my brother Jason, and my older son Weston wait ahead of us in line. All are smiling. Excited children clad in flip-flops and bathing suits talk excitedly in front of us as they wait their turn to sail in the boats.

The boats will launch from a small dock on the side of a calm, ocean inlet. To the right, the inlet leads to the ocean. But to the left, the inlet winds lazily down to a sandy beach a few miles from the dock.

I snap a few pictures and smile, thinking how much fun this is going to be for all of us.

Suddenly, Nicholas grabs my hand and starts to wail, "Mummy, I don't want to gooooo!"

"It's okay, Nicholas," I say. My cheeks flush while my mind races to think of some unbelievably brilliant plan to get this unhappy child into the boat.

"No!" he answers adamantly.

My pleasant vision of a leisurely boat ride down the inlet quickly dissolves into nothingness.

"Go ahead," I say to my husband, trying to disguise my disappointment.

I try very hard not to be angry with Nicholas. I know he is hot and tired and having trouble with this transition. He has never ridden in a paddleboat.

I hate transitions, too. I hate that life is full of them. I hate having to be resilient all of the time. I hate that my son was born with Prader-Willi syndrome. I hate that we can never escape from it. I hate that it is always me who has to accommodate.

I find a patio area beside the dock and slump into a chair. Once again, Nicholas starts to scream, but this time with glee as he notices a portable fireplace sitting on the patio. Here we settle, me scowling in my chair and Nicholas dancing around the cold, empty fireplace, pretending it's a roaring campfire keeping us warm in the sunny, eighty-degree weather.

Sulking, I watch Jason, Pete, and Weston board their paddleboat and snicker when they step into the tiny boat and it sinks deeply into the water. Burdened by the weight of these heavy passengers, the boat is now almost parallel with the water and looks as though it might start to take on water. With Jason on one side, Pete on the other, and Weston in the middle, the plastic recreational vessel sits deep in the water but manages somehow to stay afloat. The two young boat attendants push together in unison and heave the heavily laden boat out into the canal.

Like Napoleon seated between two giant soldiers, Weston begins shouting out commands: "Watch out for the birds!" "You're going too fast!" "Can I paddle?" "Go this way! Go this way!"

And like Barney Rubble and Fred Flintstone driving their Bedrock vehicles, Pete and Jason's legs become a blur as they spin the pedals of the nearly submerged boat, pumping furiously to slowly maneuver it away from the dock. A cool breeze sweeps through the patio area. Nicholas smiles brightly as he places tiny sticks into the empty fireplace. I smile.

More and more canoes and paddleboats are pushed, one after another, into the calm but unpredictable canal. Unsuspecting and inexperienced passengers receive little or no instruction on how to operate the testy vessels. Watching the scene with interest from shore, I think to myself, *This just may be more exciting than a paddleboat ride.*

Sure enough, it isn't long before a group of Chinese Americans sail by our viewing area. Slicing through the water like a torpedo toward its target, their canoe is heading directly toward my three parted family members at ramming speed. Acting quickly, Jason bravely reaches out and pushes the helpless canoe away and into the surrounding sea grass, saving our mighty threesome from a certain mishap at sea! The bewildered Asian crew looks out from the grass in disbelief, frozen with fear and still unable to operate their speedy and uncooperative canoe.

I start to laugh out loud as I realize Nicholas and I have the best seats in the house.

The hilarious spectacle continues when a crew of adventuresome but elderly passengers loads into the next paddleboat. They bravely board the vessel, smiling and waving to their family waiting on shore. Without much warning or instruction, the young attendant shoves their paddleboat abruptly out into the middle of the waterway. The ocean current has picked up speed and begins swirling around their boat. The once-happy looks on their faces quickly turn to horror as their tiny, doomed boat floats steadily downstream toward the ocean. Try as they may, their tired legs simply cannot out-paddle the swift current. They spend twenty minutes just spinning around in circles.

A good Samaritan and his son manage to maneuver out to the tiring senior citizens. But with no rope or other means to pull them, he is unable to help them. He paddles back to the launch area, screaming at the useless attendants, who idly lounge about waiting for the more skilled passengers to return to the dock while the defeated elders float farther out to sea.

I am now laughing so hard I am crying. Nicholas stops dancing around the imaginary fire, and he, too, starts to laugh.

For more than an hour, we watch the procession of hapless boats. Cooled by the sea breezes and shady trees, we watch the innocent-looking boats come viciously to life, kidnapping their unsuspecting victims and casting them into the quaint little inlet that has been transformed into turbulent rapids.

The good Samaritan finally rescues the elders. The Chinese Americans bring the canoe safely back to shore. And Weston, Pete, and Jason come back all smiles from their float down the river.

"Mummy, aren't you glad we didn't go on the boats?" Nicholas asks.

"Yes, honey, I am," I laugh, realizing that our experience this day is a lot like living with Prader-Willi syndrome. Although Nicholas and I didn't float leisurely down the river, we sure had a great ride.

—Lisa Peters

Speaking Up

My son Collin is what parents ten years ago might have called "husky," because they were trying to be kind. Parents twenty years ago probably would've said "chunky." Go back fifteen years when boldness was part and parcel of a tougher generation, and he'd likely just be called "fat." Don't ask me why he's this way. We don't have cookies in our house. He eats normal-sized portions, runs like a maniac in the park everyday, and out-climbs any monkey on the playground. And he comes from thin-as-a-rail stock. His mama is five feet three inches tall and weighs in at . . . well, you didn't think I'd tell you, did you? Let's just say, if I did tell you, you'd want to shove my face in a mud puddle on one of your fat days. His daddy can eat a whole turkey on Thanksgiving and still have room to button his thirty-one-inch jeans.

The point is, Collin's bulky size at eighteen months, putting him in size two toddler clothes, makes him look a lot older than he is. What's the problem with this? People expect a lot more out of him than he's capable of, especially when they see him in action. When he's swinging by his knuckles from the big-kid play structure at the park or sliding down the swirly slides without falling backward, or throwing a ball straight, they expect him to be able to tell them his name or answer them when they ask what color is the sky.

He can't. He can't say "hello." He can't say "please" when they ask for simple manners. Until a few weeks ago, he couldn't say "Mama." "Dada" is equally as new. My son is language-delayed. You might not think this is a special need, but let me tell you, it is. When your son stands in front of you and screams at the top of his lungs because he can't tell you what he wants but he so badly wants to be understood, it's a special need. When he melts down into a puddle of toddler tears and red-faced sobs because you simply can't understand blubber or, worse, silence, but he most certainly needs something, it's a special need.

We knew something was wrong when, by six months, Collin wasn't babbling. No gurgles, no burbles, nothing. Silence. Sure, we heard screams and shrieks when he needed something, really needed something, but other than that, we just took the compliments as they were handed to us that we had an especially easy baby because he was so quiet. Sure, he was easy. But when you are a parent, you know when something isn't right. And by twelve months, when the only actual word he said was the dog's name, we knew something wasn't right.

At our son's one-year checkup, we begged for a language referral from the pediatrician, but he wanted to wait until Collin was fifteen months old, because his receptive language skills seemed on target, if not above age level. He could, and still does, follow multistep commands and directions. I think if you asked him to get in the car, turn the ignition, and drive to the Esso station, fill up the tank, and come home, he might be able to do it. Still, ask him to say "car" and he'll stare blankly at you.

Thankfully, we'd started signing with him at around eight months old. We began with basic signs for his daily functions: eat, sleep, change, bath, and so on. Near his first birthday, he suddenly started signing back to us. We ran into a lot of resistance about the signing from some of our family and friends, who were convinced that having an alternative form of communication would discourage him from speaking to us. They thought that signing was slowing down his verbal communications development. They also thought that our not allowing Collin to watch any television was somehow denying him a language-learning opportunity. Apparently, Sesame Street and Baby Einstein are the best places for kids to learn to talk these days. Nevertheless, I held my ground and was reassured every time the pediatrician rolled his eyes at those comments and told me I was on the right track and doing the right thing by my son.

Collin's signs have been a lifesaver. I think of them as his message in a bottle, which he can send to me across the ocean from the island he's trapped on. He may not be able to tell me things, but he can show me what he means with those chubby little hands of his. It's amazing to be able to "see" what he's thinking and feeling, what he needs and wants, in this way. And when I voice the word he signs and get what he's trying to "say" right, the glowing smile of recognition on his sweet face is priceless. He's so pleased to be able to communicate his needs to me, to not be marooned on that island, that it's worth all the seemingly endless repetition of signs that we did when he was an infant and he didn't seem to be getting it.

Collin is starting speech therapy again very soon. He has been assessed twice. Initially, they thought it was a simple language delay. While such delays are fairly common in boys, it was too soon to determine the root cause and whether it was related to a cognitive problem. At his more recent assessment, his therapist felt more certain that Collin has verbal apraxia, a disorder in which, quite simply, my son knows precisely what he wants to say but has trouble saying it.

Still, we've gone through the rigmarole of getting our insurance company's approval to transfer Collin to a speech therapist closer to our home, and that has delayed the start of his therapy sessions by months. Although his first therapist was only about thirty miles away, with the traffic congestion in our Los Angeles suburb, thirty miles might as well be in Utah. I held my ground for a closer therapist, figuring that the two hours we'd be spending twice a week in the car commuting for his appointments could be much better spent playing with his peers and learning language in action. But holding out for another therapist meant another waiting list. You might be surprised to learn just how many kids are waiting for this kind of treatment. It's shocking and sad to see how many children need help.

It's also heartbreaking to see the look on strangers' faces when they expect something of your child and he doesn't deliver. When the checkout girl says, "What's your name," and your child claps in response because the woman smiled kindly, evoking a look of pity from her that she can't quite land directly in your eye but instead directs at the floor, it's hurtful. It isn't as though he's covered in leprosy spots, has an extra arm growing out of his forehead, or is exhibiting delinquent behavior; he is just not speaking.

I realize that many of my hurt feelings come from within my own soul. It isn't that I feel shame for my son; it's that I want to protect him. I fear that he'll sense he's somehow different or that he'll feel somehow less-than, and I don't want anyone to make him feel that way. I don't want him to know that he is not typical in this respect.

What he must know, instead, is that we sound out all of our words at home. That we read all the time, so much that it's become his favorite activity. That not getting his food without making some sort of sound or noise in addition to his signs means something. But I'll be darned if strangers, or anyone, will make him feel wrong for it.

Everyday I think to myself, *What did I do to cause this? He was three weeks early. Did I walk too much when I was pregnant? Did I drink too much diet soda? Is he quiet because I talk too much now? Does he just not have anything to say? Doesn't he like me?*

But in the end, I know that all of my questions and concerns and feelings about my son's language delay mean one thing. Everything I have done and do—from reading and signing with him to latching onto that one sound he makes in a day and repeating it 30 billion times—means one thing: I'm a good mother, and Collin is an exceptional child. No matter how many strangers look oddly at us or even just look twice, I cannot for one second doubt how wonderful my son is and how devoted I am to him. His toddler girth and his special needs just make him a little larger than life right now. Pretty soon, though, he'll thin out and start talking, and people will stop gawking. Even if he doesn't—even if he comes up to my chin and needs to open and close his fist, signing for milk instead of saying it aloud, when he's six years old—that's going to be okay with me. Because I know that if we keep encouraging him, Collin will reach his full potential. And I know that he is a fantastic kid and we are a fantastic family.

—*Rachel McClain*

Funny-Looking Kid

When I saw the second blue line appear on the home pregnancy test stick, I jumped up and down in the privacy of the upstairs bathroom. I hadn't expected to become pregnant so quickly, but I was thrilled from the moment I felt that first wave of queasiness rise up and take hold inside my chest.

I spent the next several months happily preparing for motherhood. My mother and I spent weeks selecting the layette. I wasn't having the kind of prenatal testing that tells the sex of the baby, so we looked for clothes and accessories that would be appropriate for either. We made regular trips to the trendiest baby stores in the area, choosing receiving blankets, tiny undershirts, and hooded towels trimmed with yellow satin piping.

We went to every baby furniture store within twenty miles in search of the perfect crib. Finally, we found it: white lacquered wood with straight slats and a rounded headboard. We pored over catalogs of special-order crib bedding, looking for something that was neither frilly nor boyish. We found a quilt made of sewn-together squares in all the colors of the rainbow with a matching bumper to protect the baby's head from banging into the crib's wooden slats.

I decorated the soon-to-be nursery with mint-green carpeting and wallpaper covered with hundreds of pastel-colored balloons: pink, yellow, sky blue, and green. I bought diapers and wipes, bottles in assorted sizes, cases of formula, and special laundry detergent that would be gentle enough to wash the baby's clothes without causing irritation.

I was filled with expectation, happy and hopeful. At night I'd sit on the couch with my husband watching television, my legs stretched out in front of me, an afghan covering my feet. Sitting there night after night, hands resting on a stomach that seemed to grow bigger by the minute, I felt content.

The baby was due in March. I watched the snow melt. The garden center on the corner replaced its displays of evergreen and tired-looking wreaths with containers of bright fuchsia flowers and lipstick-red geraniums. I saw the signs of spring as I'd never seen them before, equating them with the new life growing inside me.

After many arguments, we decided on names: Molly or Michael, both in memory of my mother's father, Morris. We took the requisite Lamaze class, although I tried not to think about the actual birth too much. The thought of all that blood and pain made me anxious. I stayed focused on the baby that would soon come into my life. I thought about becoming a mother for the first time.

On the afternoon of my due date, I started having contractions. Within an hour, they were coming faster and faster. I called my doctor, who told me to keep track of the intensity and frequency. After another hour, my water broke. I called the doctor again, and he told me to come to the hospital. I grabbed the bag I had packed weeks ago, called my parents, and we were on our way.

I lay there for several hours in a dull haze of Demerol, punctuated by nauseating cramps that became increasingly frequent and severe as the hours passed. When it was time, I pushed as hard as I could, not even trying to contain the scream as the searing pain shot through me. I felt the baby leave my body, and in a moment, it was over, as suddenly as it had begun.

"It's a girl," I heard a voice say. Molly. I realized how much I had wanted a girl, though I had told myself I would love my baby no matter what sex it was.

I looked up and saw Molly, bundled in a white blanket and tiny hat. I tried to get a closer look at her, but one of the nurses was carrying her out of the room. People seemed to be scurrying. I started feeling uneasy.

"Is she okay?" I asked.

Two nurses exchanged glances before one of them answered. "Yes, she's fine. She was a little woozy right after the birth, but she's fine now. Her Apgar scores are right where they should be."

Those were reassuring words, but I didn't feel comforted. There was something in her tone, in the atmosphere of the room, in the worried looks and whispers of the people who came and went.

"Are you sure nothing's wrong?"

"Everything's fine," I was told again.

It didn't feel like everything was fine. I had a growing sense that nothing would ever be fine again.

The next morning the pediatrician came to see me. His eyes were kind, and a feeling of dread began to rise and spread throughout my body.

"We want to run some tests," he said. He explained that Molly had some unusual characteristics that concerned him: atypical facial features, an abnormally thick tuft of hair at the base of her spine, low muscle tone. They wanted to explore the possibility of a genetic syndrome.

The dread rose up and filled my throat. I swallowed, trying to push it down so that I could speak. I had never felt so afraid. I thought that I would rather hear my own death sentence than hear that there was something wrong with my child, with my Molly.

The test results were all normal. The doctor told me to take her home, that we would discuss the next step at her two-week exam.

While I had been at the hospital giving birth, my mother had finished setting up the nursery at home. I carried Molly into the house and upstairs to her mint-green carpeted, balloon-wallpapered room. Her tiny clothes were laid out in the drawers of the dresser we'd bought to match the crib. But the happy expectation I had felt throughout my pregnancy was gone. A pervasive sense of fear and trepidation had taken its place.

Another round of tests was performed: blood work, CAT scans, X-rays, EEGs. Nothing negative was discovered. Yet, something was wrong. Molly wasn't achieving her developmental milestones. When she didn't roll over, sit up, or crawl at the normally prescribed times, the doctor suggested that we begin physical and occupational therapy and enroll her in an early-intervention program through the school district.

Life became a series of therapy sessions, meetings to discuss goals and progress, appointments with specialists—geneticists, neurologists, developmental psychologists—and more tests. I watched my baby get poked and prodded and examined and discussed. I sat across from doctors who told me she would never be normal. I left each appointment numb and dazed.

One morning, I sat in yet another doctor's waiting room, looking through the sheaf of medical records I'd picked up from the pediatrician's office. At the top of one of the pages were three letters: "FLK." They were underlined. When I met with the doctor, I showed him the page in question and asked him what the initials meant.

He cleared his throat and shifted in his seat. "That's medical slang," he said. "It means 'funny-looking kid.' Doctors write that when a child doesn't look right but they're not sure what the problem is."

Funny-looking kid. I don't remember anything he said after that. I put the papers back into my folder and left his office.

Those words reverberated in my mind many times during the first few years of Molly's life as her development continued to lag behind the normal standards. I was in a constant state of worry mixed with profound sadness.

Birthday parties reduced me to tears. Watching the other toddlers running and playing and laughing while two-year-old Molly sat on the floor, not yet able to walk, broke my heart. This wasn't what I had expected during all those months of planning and preparation. I didn't know how to live with this new reality.

I felt myself teetering on the edge of a dark and very deep hole, and I knew I didn't want to fall in. I formed a support group for other parents of children with special needs. I made friends who understood the perils of the birthday party and the despair that could descend after a visit to yet another specialist.

In time, I came to see that, in addition to having disabilities, Molly also had beautiful brown eyes, an inquisitive mind, and a loving heart. Being her mother began to change my view of life and the way I dealt with it. When my two younger children, Ethan and Lily, were born, I viewed each accomplishment, no matter how minor, as a miracle. I still do. I spend less time worrying about trivial details and more time noticing and appreciating the positive things and people in my life.

When the day came to celebrate Molly's high school graduation, the memory of that terrifying day in the delivery room eighteen years earlier had receded. I sat in the bleachers of the amphitheater with my sister, my two younger children, and their father, who is now my ex-husband. As the principal called each name, the students walked across the stage to receive their diplomas. The audience was quiet, having been asked to delay our applause until all the names had been called.

Then it was Molly's turn. I held my breath. Her teachers and aides had been rehearsing this moment for weeks, but nobody was sure how she would react when the actual time came. At the sound of her name, she started across the stage. She was wearing her cap and gown and a smile bright enough to be seen all the way from the back row. She waved her hands up and down, as she does when she's excited. The room filled with applause, but it didn't register with me at first. Then it got louder. I looked around. Despite the principal's request, the entire audience was standing, clapping their hands and cheering as Molly danced her way across the stage.

The years of doubt and pain and abandoned dreams dissolved as I saw my daughter as she truly was. This was no funny-looking kid. This was a beautiful young woman—happy, radiant, and able to inspire 5,000 people and bring them to their feet in celebration. Grabbing my sister's arm, I pulled her up from her seat and we joined in the standing ovation.

—*Ronelle Grier*

He Believed I Could Fly

"It isn't fair, Dad!" I yelled as I burst through the front door.

"Honey, didn't you win the election?"

"Yes, Dad," I spoke through sobs. "I won, but the teacher said I'm blind, so he won't let me be class president."

"What? Being partially sighted shouldn't make a difference. You are capable of becoming a leader." He patted my hand. "I'll go talk with him."

Dad left for the school, and I squared my shoulders. Because he believed in me, I had to be brave no matter what happened. While waiting, I paced and bit my nails. He finally came quietly through the door and grabbed me in a tight hug. My stomach knotted with dread.

"Pam, I tried. Your teacher is a stubborn, prejudiced man. He and the principal are determined to stick together."

My heart sank. "Then he won't let me do it?"

"No, sweetheart. I'm sorry."

Dad stroked my hair and held me as I cried into his chest. He handed me one of his big red checkered handkerchiefs.

"But I won, Dad," I gulped.

"Yes, sweetie, and that's what you need to remember."

"Then, why can't I be happy about it? I could have done the job. It hurts to have the chance to serve my classmates taken away from me."

"I know, it's a big disappointment for you." He touched my cheek. "You're still my winner, and I'm proud of you."

Dad's words helped me feel less sad about not being class president.

"Hey, I have an idea," Dad said brightly. "What about the bike you've been wanting to learn to ride?"

His confidence in me made me smile. "Let's go for it, Dad." I looked forward to another adventure!

We went to a church parking lot. Patiently, Dad taught me how to balance on the bike and steadied me while I practiced.

"Shall I let go?"

"I think so."

"You can do it." he encouraged.

I wobbled at first, but then rode smoothly down the pavement.

"You're a natural!" Dad cheered.

I could see the path before me but not clearly enough to notice the rock in the road. I ran over it and swiveled. Righting myself, I kept going.

Dad hurried up to me, chuckling. "I didn't see that rock either, or I would have moved it out of the way like I did the others. He whistled. "Wow! You didn't fall."

His praise made me glow inside.

"Now that it's over, I'm a little scared," I admitted. "Dad, what if I hit another rock that I don't see and fall?"

Dad put his arm around me. "Pam, it's like when you learned to walk. I cleared the way so you wouldn't run into anything, as I did today. Then, I let you take one step at a time. I was close by so that, if you fell, I would be near to catch you. And you did fall, but you got up and tried again. That's how it is now with riding your bike. You can pedal around, but I'll never be too far away if you need me."

I knew Dad would never leave me. He gave me the courage to eventually cycle on our residential street.

He ran along beside me and let me know if a car was coming, so I could move to the side of the road.

That evening, I heard Dad reassure Mom. "Pam already climbs trees, skates, and plays in the pond. Now she can ride a bike. We can't hold her back from experiencing life. I'll always keep an eye on her to make sure she's safe."

I rode some more with Dad's coaching, but because Mom still seemed concerned, I focused on other projects. I didn't have to ride a bike anymore; I'd accomplished it, and I could move on. Dad taught me that achievement is not a measurement of my value and that self-esteem comes from who I am within.

There were other occasions when Dad kept me out of harm's way. During our vacation on the Pacific Coast, Dad watched me while I was running up and down the beach and into the waves.

The relatives asked, "How can you let her do that?"

He shrugged. "I'll know if she is in trouble."

Once, Dad looked up and saw a perplexed, fearful expression on my face. "Honey, you aren't lost," he called. "I'm over here. Come this way, Pam."

Dad also protected me as a teen. One time, a smart aleck guy questioned him, "How can I take Pam on a date to a movie if she's blind?"

"You'll have to ask her if she'd even want to go out with you," Dad quipped. "She's the one to tell you how much she can see and whether she can follow the plot. You could fill her in, if you are willing to."

Dad told me about it later. With a lilt in his tone, he said, "The best advice I can give you is off a mayonnaise jar. Around a guy like that, "Keep cool but don't freeze." I'm sure Dad had a twinkle in his blue eyes with that one.

Even when I went away to college, I could sense Dad looking over my shoulder. I burned waffles, the first meal I fixed for my roommates. It seemed he nudged my elbow and said, "Well, we all make mistakes. Clean it up and cook one of our gourmet dinners instead."

Throughout my life, Dad let me be like a baby bird leaving the nest to try my wings, coming back if I needed to, and venturing out on my own when I was ready.

Dad allowed me to live fully. He loved and affirmed me as a unique human being.

My dad was there for me, and because of him I can fly.

—Pam Bostwick

Riding a Bike

It is a rite of passage that most children experience by the time they are six or seven years old: the simple art of riding a bike. Usually, this skill is acquired without tremendous effort. A few days or weeks spent practicing with training wheels, followed by a gentle push or two from an encouraging adult, and the child—empowered with pixie-dust belief—soars into Neverland. Victorious shouts linger in the air above the fledging cyclist. "I did it!" "Look at me!" "I can ride!" He has earned his wheels, which grants him freedom, unlimited adventure, and entrance into the free-wheeling league of his peers.

Like many other boys his age, my son got a shiny new mountain bike with training wheels for his sixth birthday. It was just like the one he'd seen on TV, with a jet-black frame and high arched silver handlebars that glistened in the sunlight.

Although the bike was emblematic of boyhood, teaching Garrett to ride was not. For a child with a developmental disability, learning to ride a bike, if it happens at all, is like a typically developing child mastering a spin on a bucking bronco. Simply trying to persuade him to try something new outside his narrow range of interests was like navigating a minefield.

"Garrett, how about trying out your new bike today?" his father asked.

His reply was almost always the same, a definitive "No!"

"Just for a little while? We could ride around the cul-de-sac like the other boys."

"I don't want to!" Even his desire to fit in with his peers wasn't enough to motivate him to try.

At times Caitlin, his older sister, tried to cajole him to be her playmate. "Garrett, do you want to ride with me?"

Having a brother with special needs robbed her of the conventional sibling relationship that I'd longed to give her when we decided to have a second child. The intrusion on her life from his presence came early, from the pre-term labor that put me to bed for ten weeks before his birth to the constant demands from his inconsolable crying after he arrived. Their differences became more apparent with each developmental milestone either missed or delayed.

Sometimes, I joined the attempt to get Garrett on his bike. "Come on, I'll jog beside you while you ride."

"Mom! I said 'no!'"

Usually, nothing convinced him to try, and if one of us pushed too hard, we were likely to land upon one of the hidden mines buried just below the surface of a child with autism.

Occasionally, when he did get on the bike, we could almost pass for a normal suburban family. His middle-aged father would run beside him, his prematurely gray hair blowing in the wind. No one paid much attention to Scott's steady hand on the bike seat to compensate for Garrett's lack of coordination and poor balance. Letting go was out of the question, even with training wheels. Still, he rode. His sister would pedal confidently ahead, weaving in and out of each driveway in the cul-de-sac, smiling and waving to her younger brother. For a few brief moments, she had the family she's always wanted.

But then the crash would come. It always did. As huge tears streamed down his face, Garrett would kick the bike and scream, "Stupid bike! I hate that bike! I am never going to ride it again!"

Mentally exhausted, we'd put the bike back into the garage. It would be several months before any of us had the fortitude or courage to try again.

Four years later, when Garrett was ten years old, I suggested that we rent bikes while vacationing in Mammoth Lakes, California. My family thought I was a little bit crazy, but they reluctantly agreed to try. We cautiously mounted the tandem bikes we chose, hoping Garrett would be able to balance behind Scott but knowing that a slight change in the direction of the wind would be enough to blow us off course. After a shaky start, we developed a rhythm and rode through the winding paths of the Sierra Nevada Mountains. Scott and Garrett took the lead, and Caitlin and I followed close behind. With each push of the pedal, we ventured closer to being a typical family.

Buoyed by the success we enjoyed in Mammoth, Caitlin and I rented bikes at our next stop in Yosemite Valley.

"I'll race you back to the campsite," Caitlin said.

When we arrived, I asked Garrett, "Do you want to ride my bike?"

"Yeah! I want to try."

Caitlin shot me a look with her piercing dark brown eyes and said, "I can't believe you suggested that." This is the same child who bungee jumps and has gone parasailing; the former six-year-old who asked me, "What does it mean when people say, 'Don't count your chickens before they hatch'?"—then came up with an answer before I had a chance to respond, "I know, because one of them might be twins!" However, that kind of optimism was long before autism had set up camp in our family.

Despite Caitlin's desire not to let our peaceful campsite turn into a nuclear meltdown, we let Garrett try. He zipped up his tennis shoes and struggled to fasten the buckle on his bike helmet, then climbed onto the bike. I jogged beside him and held onto the seat to get him going. We went a few feet before he fell. I braced myself for the explosion, but instead he picked himself up and said, "First you have to learn how to fall." Then he carefully lifted the bike and remounted. Once again, I held his seat and ran beside him.

"Let go, Mom! Let go!"

I didn't. I couldn't risk that he would fall so hard that he would give up again.

"Mom! If I am ever going to do it, you have to let go!"

He was right. I had to let go. Not just of the bike, but of him. Even with his special challenges, he deserves a chance to make it on his own in life. So I let go. And amazingly, he rode. He wound his way through the campground, up and down each row of trailers and tents. He fell several times, but each time he got right back up again, brushed off the dirt, and rode some more, until he'd made his way back to our campsite.

Almost on cue, a boy from the neighboring campsite came over and asked, "Do you want to ride bikes?"

"Sure," Garrett said as he shrugged his shoulders, seemingly perplexed by the sudden interest from a peer.

With a lump in my throat, I watched as they put on their helmets, climbed on their bikes, and took off through the forest.

Because of his autism, words sometimes fail Garrett in the awkwardness of social exchange. Yet, in this setting, words weren't necessary. As the chain rubbed against metal and the tires crushed gravel on the asphalt road, the rhythmic language of the bike was enough. With Half Dome's sheer granite wall looming overhead like a protective ancient god and among towering pines that have weathered many storms, Garrett was just a typical boy riding a bike.

—Wendy Hill Williams

One in Eight Hundred

Twins?

The technician swirled the probe over my three-month pregnancy bump. "Yep. There's one head . . ." she paused, swirled again. "And there's the other."

And there I was. Dazed and confused. At twenty-nine, I had a five-year-old son and a two-year-old daughter, and I'd just doubled the numbers.

But that wasn't the end of the surprises. My twin daughters were born on Easter Sunday. The next morning, the pediatrician walked into my room and announced that one of the babies had Down syndrome. Just like that.

Twenty-five years later, I read that the American College of Obstetricians and Gynecologists recommended every pregnant woman be offered a test to screen for Down syndrome and other chromosomal defects. The article stated that about one in 800 babies is born with Down syndrome, a condition in which an extra chromosome causes mental retardation; a characteristic broad flat face, almond-shaped eyes, small head, short stature, and "webbed" fingers and toes; and often serious heart defects.

Sarah is more than mental retardation and a set of certain physical features. She is so much more than an extra chromosome and a "condition." Fortunately, she has no heart defects, except when her boyfriend tells her that he's thinking about his old girlfriend. Sarah does not think she is cute or beautiful—she *knows*. Ask her, and she will tell you she is *gorgeous*! As for her head, I assure you, it's not microscopic, and however smaller than "normal" her cranium might be, it houses a stubborn and active brain. Some mornings, for example, Sarah refuses to get on the school bus with her siblings. Other days, she refuses to get off. And when she makes a wardrobe decision—for example, donning a purple teeshirt, red shorts, and black ankle boots—there's no convincing her that she's a fashion nightmare. Her response to my suggestions for changing into something more coordinated is an emphatic, arms-folded, "I'm wearing this."

Sarah writes stories on her computer, her AlphaSmart, and any notebook she can find. She's an avid word-search puzzle fan and works the most complicated ones I've ever seen. She folds clothes, empties the dishwasher, helps me cook, sets the table, vacuums her bedroom and cleans her bathroom, rakes and sweeps outside.

She loves to go bowling with her pink bowling ball and shoes. She is wild about going to Louisiana State University games with her father and loves game days. If I'm not wearing purple and gold the day of an LSU game, she'll politely remind me that I need to change. She and I hang out in book stores, where she cruises the aisles in search of the latest additions to her book collections. Her movie DVD and music CD collections are extensive, some purchased with her own money from her own job. One of her favorite songs is "I Can Only Imagine," by Mercy Me, which she listens to raptly. She has her own cell phone and knows how to call anyone at anytime (ask her siblings). She orders her own food at restaurants, adores her nieces, and can spell better than many of the high school juniors I teach.

Sarah reads and studies her Bible almost every day. And those who have witnessed Sarah singing in church will attest that it is an extraordinary experience. Sometimes she signs along with the songs. Her love for the Lord transforms her when she is celebrating with song and prayer; her face and eyes glisten.

Sarah sometimes tells me the moon looks like a banana or a pizza. She is equally observant about other things in her world. She talks to me about Bailey, my grandson and her nephew, who went to heaven when he was a month old, about how happy he is with her Meemaw and Papa in heaven.

For the record, Sarah has the small ears and crooked little fingers characteristic of DS. Like other people with DS, she also has forearms that are not exactly proportional and is missing the simian crease in her palms. Given that adults with DS tend to be below-average in height and that Sarah has the misfortune of having a short mother (four feet, eleven inches), we're glad she's four feet, five inches.

Here's another fact for the record: Sarah's twin, Shannon, is as vivacious, beautiful, interesting, and stubborn as her womb mate. But she does not have Down syndrome or heart defects or mental retardation.

Such are the odds. Sarah is among the one in every eight-hundred people who has Down syndrome; Shannon is one of the 799 who do not. But what guarantees do those 799 people have that nothing will ever happen to them for the rest of their lives that will not, in one way or another, damage them mentally, physically, or emotionally? Any one of my other four children could, by virtue of an illness or accident, be rendered as "disabled" or "retarded" as their sister—or even more so.

Because of Sarah, my other children learned sympathy and empathy at early ages. Some kids at school would ask if they were retarded like their sister, and sometimes adults would make the dumbest statements, often in front of Sarah. We'd have to remind people that having DS did not mean she was deaf or that she did not understand scorn.

Once, a new neighbor asked me which of my five kids were twins. When I indicated Sarah and Shannon, the lady looked at them and then at me and said (I couldn't make this up), "Are you sure?"

Another genius, when I was having the girls' pictures taken at a studio, pointed to Sarah and said to me, "What's wrong with her?"

I choked out, "Nothing," stifling what I wanted to reply—"What's wrong with you for asking?"

Two years ago, the local Association for Retarded Citizens hosted a Christmas dance at the VFW hall. Several of Sarah's work friends arrived there at the same time we did. They were all dressed in their holiday glitz and glitter; Sarah had opted for a Christmas tee-shirt. One of her friends, Ann, held the door open and excitedly welcomed us in. I told her how pretty she looked, and her comment to me, quite matter-of-factly, was, "Yes, I do look pretty tonight." Then off she went to join her friend. Sarah and her friends were delighted with the down-the-bayou band, the cafeteria tables and folding chairs, a meal served without fanfare or artistic presentation, and a choice of three flavors of canned sodas. There was so much joy with so few trappings. They slow-danced to foot-tapping music, boogied to the huggy songs, and twirled solo. They were having fun.

I smiled, but my heart was touched with sadness. The sadness wasn't for Ann or Sarah. Their self-esteem didn't need a makeover. My sadness was for those of us who fail to see our own beauty and for those who may never see it in Ann and Sarah.

If I had a choice, would I want Sarah to be "normal"? Well, of course. (And I'll save that definition of normal for another time.) For years, I was terribly angry with God. God, who could raise Lazarus from the dead, couldn't take away a chromosome? Wouldn't fix my child?

But God didn't fix Sarah. God used Sarah to fix me.

As he in his infinite wisdom knew, Sarah is perfect just the way she is, and her life is awash in goodness. At times, she'll look at me and say, "I love my life."

—Christa B. Allan

Greater Than the Achievement

The cream-colored certificate is smaller than the achievement it represents. The raised, golden seal at the top confirms its significance. Heavy, black Old English letters give it a look of importance. Its authenticity is verified by four signatures at the bottom. My nineteen-year-old son's name is prominently displayed in the center.

"Kevin, we're going to frame it!" I say, my face beaming with pride.

"It's just a piece of paper, Mom."

"Aren't you excited?" I asked, knowing my son doesn't experience emotions like others do. "You should be proud! This piece of paper demonstrates many years of blood, sweat, and tears."

"Mom, it doesn't make me sweat or cry, and I'm not bleeding." Kevin didn't understand my analogy.

He takes speech literally, which sometimes makes communicating difficult.

I stood on my tippy toes and reached up to hug his neck. "Kevin, I am so proud of you!"

He cringed, took a giant leap back, and then disappeared into his room. In my own excitement, I'd forgotten that my son doesn't like to be touched.

Staring at the piece of paper in my hand, I thought about how far my son has come over the years.

"Nurse, we need to prepare her for a C-section immediately."

"What's wrong? Is it the fetal heart monitor? You said I wasn't in labor," my voice trembled. I felt no pain.

As the orderly rushed me on a gurney down the long corridor, Dr. Anderson's words raced through my mind, "The baby is in distress." During the wee hours of that May morning, my precious baby boy greeted the world. The umbilical cord had wrapped around his neck as he tried to push past the placenta, which was covering the birth canal. He was deprived of oxygen, and we almost lost him. But he was a survivor—destined to be in this world—and he chose me to be his mother. I never suspected that my son's traumatic birth could result in such a challenging infancy, nor did I ever imagine he would have permanent neurological complications. Kevin was a colicky baby, and he preferred his swing over being held. He didn't respond well to touch. While most mothers enjoy rocking their babies to sleep, I had to bundle up my son on the coldest of nights and buckle him into his car seat to drive him to sleep.

At age twenty-seven, I found myself divorced, working full-time, and raising an eight-month-old baby who required much more time and patience than a typical baby. Kevin was my pride and joy, but it took all the energy I could muster to care for him.

My Aunt Gina provided daycare in her home for several children, including Kevin. I will always be grateful to her for keeping my son, because nobody else would. By the time he was two years old, he was a danger to other kids and had to be watched carefully. His tantrums went far beyond the "terrible twos."

"It happened again," Gina said. "I turned my back for a minute, and Kevin climbed into the playpen and pounced on Katie."

"Was it worse than when he bit Alex?" I asked, not wanting to hear the answer.

Gina hesitated, then replied, "Yes. Katie looked as if a cat had scratched her all over."

My head dropped in shame and my eyes filled with tears. On the way home, I asked myself the same question I'd asked many times before: *What was wrong with my son?*

At family or holiday gatherings, I was often asked to leave early due to Kevin's outrageous outbursts. My son's conduct was increasingly disturbing, and I had no idea how to help him—or myself. Sobbing became my private way of dealing with feelings of guilt, worry, and exhaustion.

First grade is supposed to be an exciting milestone for children. Not so for my son. Teachers were baffled by his behavior, and school conferences began immediately.

"Kevin breaks all of his crayons and shreds his paper," Mrs. McGee advised me with concern. "And he is having great difficulty in the cafeteria."

"School is a new routine. He doesn't like change," I explained.

"He spits his milk all over the other kids and rips his Styrofoam tray into little pieces. He rocks back and forth and thumps his head on the table."

"Give him time," I pleaded, assuring her Kevin would adjust.

But I knew something was wrong; I just didn't know what. Kevin couldn't explain to us that the clanging of dishes and utensils made him anxious. He couldn't tell us that the chaos of kids running around, chattering, and laughing, made him ache inside. He suffered in silence and continued to do so year after year in any crowded place.

"Perhaps he is depressed," his pediatrician suggested. "Let's try anti-depressant medication."

A neurologist advised, "This is the worse case of ADHD I have ever seen. I will prescribe Ritalin."

Nothing helped. When others couldn't handle Kevin, I had to miss work. I was at the end of my rope; the possibility of losing my job, while living paycheck to paycheck, loomed like a dark cloud over my head.

In retrospect, I'm surprised school personnel never suggested special education, but they didn't. Getting Kevin placed in a self-contained classroom became my biggest battle; I fought it all the way to the board of education. I searched the Internet. I read books. I did everything I could to empower myself with the knowledge necessary to fight for my son in the public school system. I attended meetings where I was the only person representing Kevin, surrounded by school officials who insisted they knew my son better than I did.

"There is nothing wrong with your son. He is just lazy." The words of school personnel infuriated me! These supposedly trained professionals failed miserably in their responsibility to provide education and guidance to my child.

After nearly a year of sheer agony, I finally won the battle when Kevin was placed in a self-contained, special education classroom.

My heart broke each day as Kevin entered school, slumped over in misery, with sad brown eyes staring down at the floor. He lived in fear of the inevitable: loud bells ringing, the hustle and bustle of lunch and recess, kids relentlessly poking fun at him.

Most mothers can't wait for their children to come home from school in the afternoon, filled with excitement and sharing stories. I couldn't wait for my son to come home crying to the safe haven of his mother. I fully expected him to quit school once he was of legal age.

Then, when Kevin was ten years old, I became cautiously optimistic when I found a pediatric neurologist who was interested enough in Kevin to listen and to fully assess him. The lengthy medical questionnaire in itself demonstrated Dr. Nelson's qualifications and knowledge. She spent a great deal of time reviewing the questionnaire I had completed as well as Kevin's medical records and school records. After Kevin was given an electroencephalogram (EEG), which tests brain activity, we had our first appointment.

"Explain to me your concerns relating to Kevin," Dr. Nelson said.

"He has great difficulty in school—not only with academics but also with behavior. He is in fifth grade with a kindergarten reading level. He destroys his supplies. He gets lost when changing classes; the noisy cafeteria panics him. He goes through trash cans, fills his pockets with metal objects from the playground. He completely exasperates his teachers and is unable to make friends." I continued, naming everything I could think of but certain, when I'd finished, that I had left out pertinent information.

Dr. Nelson turned to Kevin, who was in the corner coloring a picture of a car he had sketched. "Kevin, if we had to leave this building right now because of a fire, what would you do?"

"Finish my picture," he replied, never looking up.

Attempting to provide good reason why Kevin would stay in a fire just to finish a picture, I said, "He is extremely preoccupied with cars. He draws and colors them with great detail. As a matter of fact, all he talks about is cars."

"How is Kevin's behavior at home? Do you notice any bizarre habits?" It was obvious that Dr. Nelson had concern for my son.

"Yes, I notice a lot that seems odd. He will not wear certain fabrics or shirts with collars, buttons, or long sleeves. He doesn't like to be touched, and if his routine changes in the least, he becomes hysterical.

He frequently uses his fingernails to scrape bars of soap and candle wax. He cannot tolerate noise; he barks like a dog; he spins things incessantly; and he constantly twists his hair," I replied, hoping these details would help.

Dr. Nelson was quiet, as if absorbing information, assembling all the pieces of a puzzle.

"His fascination with fire is beginning to scare me. I woke up to the smell of burning plastic the other night and found Kevin in his room with his matchbox cars meticulously lined up, setting them on fire," I said, feeling as if I were betraying my son.

"Kevin, can you look me in the eyes when I talk to you?" the doctor asked.

"I guess," he replied, without looking up from his coloring. Kevin never says "yes" or "no"; it's always "I guess" or "I don't know."

Dr. Nelson was exceptionally thorough, and after more than two hours, I finally discovered what was wrong with my son.

"Joy, it is my professional opinion that your son has Asperger's syndrome." I could hear the compassion in her voice. "He feels as though he is visiting from a foreign country; he doesn't understand our language or gestures."

She thoughtfully explained the diagnosis. "It is a pervasive developmental disorder, an autism spectrum disorder with a range of conditions characterized by abnormalities of social interaction and communication. People with Asperger's syndrome have severe difficulties understanding how to interact socially."

"Is this why he has learning disabilities?"

"No. Kevin's EEG shows complex partial seizure activity in his brain. His learning disabilities result from brain damage due to the lack of oxygen at birth, which in all probability also caused his epilepsy."

The room was closing in around me as I soaked up her words like a sponge. I wasn't a bad mother, after all. This had to be the best day of my life—a real diagnosis. What a relief!

Not only did I become an expert in special education and learning disabilities, I also became an expert on Asperger's syndrome and epilepsy, and began to understand my child in a way I never had before. I was better able to relate to Kevin and to help him. I wasn't just his mother; I was also his advocate. And I was determined to pull him out of his own little world and into ours to the greatest extent possible.

Now, I held in my hand something I never thought I would: a piece of paper—my son's high school diploma.

Unlike most mothers, I was unable to experience the pride of watching my son walk across the stage to receive his diploma. Kevin had chosen not to participate in the commencement, due to the crowd and noise involved with the ceremony. Nevertheless, we sent out beautiful announcements, and I proudly display a photograph of him wearing his cap and gown in our home.

Kevin has struggled throughout his life thus far, suffering in isolation and feeling like a social outcast. Adulthood will not be easy, but he is making a positive start.

His persistence in earning his diploma has paid off. He's found full-time employment and received two salary increases in only five months. Better yet, it is his dream job—he is a lube technician who works on vehicles all day. My heart sings when I see him leave for work with a smile on his face and his big brown eyes sparkling with pride.

Although I know the path ahead will be strewn with rocks and sometimes lonely for Kevin, my worries have diminished. I know my son. He has the determination and courage necessary to survive in this grueling world. For that and for the many ways in which Kevin has enriched my life, I am grateful. And I am so thankful that my uniquely abled son chose me to be his mother.

—Vivian Joy Phillips

On Patrol

Kurt and I stopped at the gymnasium door to get our bearings. Twenty fifth-graders were lined up at the front, with orange patrol belts angled over their shoulders and buckled at their waists. The remaining elementary students entered single file and sat on the floor to watch the ceremony.

This was not my thirteen-year-old's normal time at school. We had walked the few blocks after lunch, our shoes crunching the gathering leaves that had dropped along the curbs just a couple of weeks into September. Our visit today was for a patrol guard ceremony. Kurt would be sworn in as a "special" patrol guard—a rare opportunity for him to give back, perhaps small to the world, but large for him.

At three years old, Kurt had developed Lennox-Gastaut syndrome, a severe form of epilepsy. He went through seven years of uncontrolled seizures while the neurologists and his dad and I tried to find the right combination of medicines. Our lives nearly collapsed three years ago when a drug-induced coma finally stopped most of the seizures but almost took his life. I had wondered then if we would ever see a day like this one.

Kurt has come a long way since then, but the disorder has still left him with a load of problems that have made school and socializing a challenge. Sickly thin, with a blond tousle of hair, he had double vision and a damaged foot. His slurred speech was difficult to understand until you got to know him, and academically, he was about five years old. In addition, medications and daily split-second seizures caused distracted and argumentative behavior.

Because of Kurt's medical and developmental disabilities, he was home-schooled, had speech and physical therapies at a center, and then attended public school three mornings a week so he could socialize with other kids.

"Let's go over there," I pointed to the patrol lineup. "Come on." I touched my son's shoulder.

Kurt was hesitant at first, covering his mouth with his hand and lowering his chin to his chest before taking off. His left foot dropped as he walked. When he spied the table of badges, he veered directly for them. That was his perk for being in patrol. He would wear a badge, just like his big brother had when he was in patrol. Just like his younger brother, Kelly, too; they were both in fifth grade because we had held Kurt back.

My shoulders tensed, always on guard, but my voice stayed calm. "Kurt, they'll give you your badge when it's your turn." With a little urging, he left reluctantly. His behavior was unpredictable, and I was relieved he hadn't picked up a badge and refused to let go.

His teacher, Mr. Fuller, a trim man with buzzed-cut hair, greeted us.

Kurt, with his head still down, let his eyes dart above his glasses to glance at his teacher, then quickly watched the floor again. A barely audible "Hi" crossed his lips.

Mr. Fuller arranged Kurt in line for the swearing-in ceremony while I took position at the back of the noisy gym with the other parents. Smiling, I watched Kurt standing in line waiting patiently for his badge. This was good. After the coma three years ago, he had to relearn how to stand and walk. We had no idea what this kid could accomplish.

But I had no expectations for his behavior. I didn't know if Kurt would continue to stand in line as he was doing or if he would run away or lie on the floor. I didn't take my eyes off him; my muscles tensed, ready to bolt if necessary. Ceremonies and events like this were hold-my-breath, hope-for-the-best, but plan-for-the-worst events. What I did know was that Kurt admired the men and women who wore badges and who made sure the rest of us were safe.

My son's teacher approached, "Would you like me to walk up with Kurt when his name is called?"

"Yes, that's a good idea. Thank you."

When Kurt, accompanied by an aide, had started in the fifth grade classroom, Mr. Fuller showed no reservations about the fact that my son was far behind the rest of the students. After a week of school, he said Kurt was interacting in class. I was encouraged by my son's behavior and grateful for this teacher's openness to the challenge. Kurt's dad and I wanted him to have time in a regular classroom, known as "mainstreaming" or "inclusion," rather than separated into a special education class. This gave Kurt a chance to be with typical kids, a rare occurrence for kids with disabilities as severe as my son's, and it gave "typical" students a chance to interact with a student like Kurt.

I watched Kurt step out of line when he spotted his younger brother a few students down. Kelly was also being sworn in during the ceremony. They talked for a few seconds, and then Kurt got back into position.

Just before the ceremony was scheduled to begin, the special education teacher, Sue Moore, greeted me. Kurt went to her room for half an hour each day to play board games with the other special education students.

The kids quieted when Principal Murray's voice came over the microphone, welcoming the group and introducing the two officers from the police department.

One of the officers spoke to the future patrol guards. "It's your duty to help students cross safely at the street corners."

Kurt wasn't capable of crossing the street on his own. So, instead, he would help at the main doors after lunch, opening the doors for visitors or students coming in from recess.

"Once you're sworn in, you'll be authorized safety guards for the police department," the officer said.

Then the two uniformed men stood behind the table set with all the badges, and worked in tandem to announce the name of each student and hand out the badges.

Kurt did exactly what he was supposed to do. Mr. Fuller gave him the "go" when his name was called, and Kurt walked up, got his badge, shook hands with the officer, and walked back to the line. He held the coveted badge in the palm of his hand, peering down at it with a huge smile across his face.

"Doesn't it make you want to cry?" Mrs. Moore whispered as she leaned toward me.

"Oh, yes. I'm so proud."

My eyes widened and my shoulders relaxed as I took in a deep breath and the scene before me. My head filled with possibilities. Seeing Kurt do a new activity was as exciting as when he was an infant and smiled for the first time or a toddler taking his first steps. New accomplishments, however small, were a welcome surprise. While it is a given for the typical child to reach each developmental milestone, those markers were thrown out for Kurt. However, his dad and I still expected him to learn new skills, and we sought opportunities for him to do so.

After the ceremony, I gathered Kurt and Kelly by the American flag and took their picture. Both boys stood proudly with their new badges on their belts. Usually, teachers and aides, doctors and nurses, and his parents and brothers helped Kurt, guarding him during a seizure or assisting with the day-to-day tasks he was unable to do for himself. The people in Kurt's life have been his personal patrol guards, diligent in keeping him safe and meeting his needs. Helping others would be a new responsibility for Kurt.

A few weeks later, my opportunity to see Kurt patrolling presented itself. As I walked up the sidewalk to bring Kelly's forgotten homework, the door opened.

"Mom!" Kurt smiled, wearing his orange belt with shiny badge. "What are you doing here?"

"Kelly forgot some homework that was due today." I paused long enough to explain before walking to Kelly's classroom.

After dropping off the papers, I stopped down the hall to observe Kurt without being seen. He stood at the ready, watching outside with his head up and his grin visible without his hand covering it. With quick determination, Kurt pushed the heavy door open, moving aside and holding it with outstretched arm. Two girls entered from the playground.

"Ah-ha!" Kurt said. I watched proudly as my son let the door shut and waited for the next opportunity to help.

—Donna Karis

Me and My Beautiful Mother

Men have always followed her with their eyes as if she were a celebrity, which in a way she is. Mom has just arrived to visit me in Oregon, and we're out for lunch. Even the young men at the bar turn their heads as we make our way to our table on the outdoor patio of the restaurant. Piped-in music competes with sparrows squabbling in a nearby tree.

Here we are: Mom in her heavy agate and gold jewelry, warm auburn hair highlighted just so—no off-shades of blue for her—and dressed in a turquoise golf ensemble. And me, in jeans, Birkenstocks, and my hair down around my shoulders in a middle-aged free-for-all.

Her current surname is Bird, and that is what she reminds me of, hollow bones hidden under tasteful layers of Estée Lauder. At seventy-three, her blue-gray eyes still don't miss much, and she often hums "Clair de Lune," which she once played on the piano.

She orders Absolut on the rocks. I order diet soda.

How I can be her daughter?

Mom smoothes back her short coif, which reminds me of falcon feathers, all layered and earth-toned.

"I'm trying to learn to do it myself," she says when I tell her I like it.

"You look great," I say.

Growing up, I treasured her dark auburn hair, not caring that she plastered it with red henna. I thought her tanned body was strong and athletic, even when her stomach got a little poochy. And although she complained that she had to wear man-sized gloves, I was in love with my mother's hands. I grew up watching her play everything from "Arabesque" to "Ebb Tide," Beethoven to boogie-woogie. Her reach was more than an octave and a half, and I wanted to play just like she did.

As an infant, I'd contracted polio, which paralyzed my left arm and hand. Despite weekly lessons, the most piano I ever played was the treble clef, or right hand. The left hand bass line wasn't a possibility, and I hated not being able to play much beyond beginning pieces. Mom never understood why piano was so frustrating to me.

But then, in many other ways, we've never been much alike. She likes to shop, cook, and golf. I'd rather sew my own clothes than go to a mall, and I'm an ambivalent cook. Golf? Please.

She must be reading my mind.

"Dave's (my brother-in-law) taking me for nine holes tomorrow afternoon," she says.

Then she cups her hand around her mouth, like a child telling a secret, and the back of her knuckles draw my attention. I glance at my hands in search of—what? Liver spots? No, that's not it. But something's different. And Mom says, "Don't tell, but I'm not as interested in golf as I was before the accident."

The Accident. That's what she calls the day, several years ago, at an Alameda, California, yacht club, when a large puppy, leash trailing, raced circles around Mom's legs. The leash tripped her, and she fell, face first, knocking out her front teeth. It was the day emergency neck surgery saved her life but severe spinal-cord bruising left her a temporary quadriplegic. The day she began months-long stays at hospitals and rehab facilities, trying to regain her muscle use and bodily functions. The day she went from a capable woman to someone who could barely write her name.

Suddenly, I wonder why no one in my family has ever given my bout with polio any kind of title. Officially, it was known as the Polio Epidemic of 1952. That year, in Phoenix, Arizona, thousands of people—plus yours truly, eight months old—contracted the feared disease. I was so young when the disease struck that I don't remember being any other way, and Mom herself was young, barely seventeen. I had bulbar polio, the most severe type, but because I was an infant, only my arm suffered permanent paralysis. Mom went along with the advice of the time: focus on the positive. Parents, mine included, told kids like me to try hard and to keep working, and we could do anything we wanted to do. In my family, there was also an unspoken "anything within reason."

Not only that, but my music-teacher grandmother thought she knew just what "within reason" meant. When I was in fifth grade she decided I would play the cornet. In theory, it's possible to play the cornet using one hand. As she pointed out, Louis "Satchmo" Armstrong held his trumpet with one hand and wiped his sweaty brow with the other. I tried playing it, and soon found out that just because something is possible doesn't mean it should be done. I ditched the cornet.

Mom raises a glass to toast her visit to the Northwest. "Here's to a great visit."

I lift my diet soda and smile. And try to figure out what I'm noticing about those hands.

As an adult, when I'd asked Mom to tell me about the days when I was first diagnosed and treated, she balked. Finally, she said, "But that's all over now. Why talk about the past?" I knew she meant I ought to get busy doing anything I wanted within reason and to quit asking painful questions.

The waiter brings her raw oysters and me half a chef's salad. Mom asks for a refill on her drink, and the divide between us yawns longer, wider, and deeper.

Mom's hand trembles awkwardly as she brings the half shell to her lips. *Funny,* I think, *she won't talk about my disability but talks about hers freely.*

Then I remember: in 1952, many still believed that infantile paralysis was spread by dirty, poor, and ignorant people. Children were banned from public swimming pools. Mothers were accused of poor sanitation or bad hygiene if their children fell ill.

Polio does spread through feces, but more privileged children contracted polio because they had limited immunity. In the two years just before the Salk and Sabin vaccines wiped out the epidemics in 1954, misinformation prevailed, causing panic every summer. My teenaged mother must have been terrified. In her mind, she'd caused my illness. Would I have been okay if she'd kept me indoors? Had she put me at risk by not sterilizing everything? Did she somehow cause the sickness that changed me forever? The weight of such regret must have almost smothered her.

When I was around eight or nine, I remember her crying in the middle of the night after she and Dad had been out drinking. She sobbed again and again, "It's my fault she got sick. All my fault." She wouldn't have admitted this if she hadn't been tipsy, but that night I decided never to do anything to make her unhappy, ever. I'd already caused so much damage. But despite my best efforts, there was always something melancholy about my mother.

Since The Accident, she's looked even sadder. Her once exuberant shopping sprees, family dinners, and golfing junkets seem not to satisfy as they once did. And her beauty has faded: her chin a little too sharp, that buttery, olive skin criss-crossed with lines. She has to draw on her eyebrows. I stare at her when she's busy looking elsewhere and think of what I've inherited. That grimace. The sigh she makes when she's not getting her way. The habit we both have of picking at our thumbnails.

Mom sets her napkin down. "I'm treating you," she says, and her wide easy smile shines her fake, almost-perfect front teeth my way.

When she signs the credit slip, I finally figure out what I've been noticing. Her hand, slow and deliberate, writes her name. Her knuckles are more like dimples than the mannish bumps I recall. No knuckles. Now I understand. My "polio" hand looks a lot like her "accident" hand, down to the way the thumb curves back too far and the way her fingers shiver when she spreads them. We are more alike now than we've ever been.

I've ached for Mom to talk to me about those days, that time when I stopped being a normal kid just learning to walk and turned into the person I am now. Today, that wish tugs at me, like a child who won't stop interrupting. I'm burning to tell her all this, but I can't and I know it.

I long to connect with my mother, to peer into her soul and to have her, in turn, peer into mine. To tell her how much I love her. To ask how we've written on each others' lives this day, this moment. To grasp hands—different, yet alike—and pray for the sick or give thanks for the chance to do lunch. It seems impossible, this connection, as improbable as restoring an umbilical cord. I could stare at my salad, or I could marvel at the beauty of motherhood. Suddenly, the sparrows fly off, and I lift my head to smile at my beautiful mother.

—Linda S. Clare

Disorderly Conduct

I opened the door to urgent pounding. It was almost 9:00 P.M., and Benn, my son's friend, stood in the porch light. Benn is tall and slender, a raggedy, homeless youth of twenty-two who'd been camping in our shed for several months. I'd started to tell him that Joshua wasn't home when he announced, "Your son is in jail. I thought ya oughta know."

His announcement hit me like whiplash, pitching me into the path of a collision I'd seen coming for years but could do nothing to stop.

Benn had few details, even though he'd been with Joshua in the cemetery when the police arrived. Benn had the common sense to leave the scene. But Joshua walked right up to the officer and offered to tell him what he'd been doing. That's the way his brain works. He's not someone who can tolerate the calm before the storm. He has to head right into the wind. It was the same when he was younger and nine or ten kids camped out on our lawn in summer, playing monster hide-and-seek in the dark. Joshua always had to be the monster hiding in the shadows. He needed to be the one who controlled the scariness. Even at nineteen, that hadn't changed.

Several years before he was arrested in the cemetery, I had been the first one to report my son's behavior to the police. He was in the fourth grade. Twice that year he'd started fires in the alley behind our house. The first time, he showed some younger boys how to light a fire with a magnifying glass. I grounded him for a month. Then I confiscated the magnifier and threw out all the matches in the house. I thought the fire chapter was closed. A few months later, the father of one of the younger boys caught them at it again. This time, Joshua had chosen a more secluded spot in the alley—under the neighbor's pickup. I needed reinforcements.

I called the police department's youth diversion officer for help. Maddy suggested "sentencing" Joshua to community service. It wasn't necessary to go through the court, she said. She volunteered to work with him herself. She counseled him once a week at the police station. Then the two of them chose a service project for the day, activities like folding brochures, weeding the cemetery, painting over graffiti, and serving dinner to the homeless.

Joshua loved community service, and he loved Maddy. After a month of giving back to the community, he no longer played with fire. I can't explain why, except to say that grounding, time outs, and gold stars never impressed Joshua, but on several significant occasions, police involvement did.

At fifteen, Joshua was diagnosed with Asperger's syndrome, a brain disorder that limits his ability to recognize and respond to social cues. Joshua can't read people or predict how they might view his odd behavior. He is not by nature a loner; he has always craved friendships. The older he got, however, the quicker his friends tired of him. The teen years, when other kids sought the approval of their peers, were especially lonely for Joshua. So, at sixteen, when he came home one day and announced that he'd met a new friend named Kip, I was happy for him. I told him to invite Kip over so Dad and I could meet him. But Kip never wanted to stop by.

Then Joshua showed up with a laptop. He said Kip gave it to him. Joshua told us his friend had received a new computer and no longer needed the laptop. I should have been more suspicious.

A week later, I received a call from Kip's mother. She said her son had some new items in his room, a boom box and a cell phone. Kip told her that Joshua had given them to him.

"Those things didn't come from Joshua," I said. "But what about Kip's laptop? Do you mind that he gave it to Joshua?"

"What laptop?" the woman asked.

I told her what Joshua told me.

"Look," she said, her tone hinting at accusation, "just so you know, I'm going to call the police and report these items—*which*, I suspect, are *stolen*. I *will* mention the laptop."

Joshua and I turned the computer in at the police station that afternoon.

A few days later, Officer Holstrum, the police liaison at the high school, found Joshua and me working in the backyard. The officer told us the laptop belonged to him. It had disappeared from his desk at school. Holstrum wanted Joshua to tell him what he knew.

"I didn't take it," Joshua began. "Kip gave it to me."

"Did you think it might be stolen?" asked Officer Holstrum.

"Yeah, I did," Joshua admitted. "But Kip said he'd destroy it if I didn't take it."

"Did you see any files on it?"

"I didn't read them. I cleaned them all off. I just wanted a computer to play games."

Holstrum explained that Joshua could be charged with receiving stolen property. It was to his benefit, however, that he was being honest.

"You shouldn't believe everything people tell you, Joshua," said the policeman.

Joshua's view of the world skewed increasingly paranoid after that. He suffers from a balloon-popping level of anxiety that he copes with by assuming the menacing bluster of a gang member.

It must have been a year after the Kip incident that I got a call at work. "The freakin' cops took my gun!" Joshua screamed into the phone.

He was still hysterical when I pulled up twenty minutes later in front of the house. By the time my husband arrived, I had been able to unearth an outline of what had set Joshua off.

Joshua was always fascinated with guns. Rich and I don't like them, so we never let our kids have even toy weapons to play with. We explained to them repeatedly that, in our post-Columbine world, toy guns could be nearly as dangerous as real ones. Joshua didn't believe us. He liked the power he felt when he played cops and gangsters.

That day, he had traded an old board game to a neighbor child for a brightly colored, plastic pistol.

He painted the pistol black with a felt marker and took it into the alley. That is where a neighbor saw a six-foot, dark-skinned "man" clothed in black, sighting down the barrel of a gun, and called the police.

Joshua, oblivious to his effect on the neighborhood, continued his pretend target practice until three police cruisers veered into the alley, one from each end of the block and one from a driveway that cut directly from the street to the gravel track. Six officers swung out of the cruisers, and ducking behind the open doors, pointed their weapons at Joshua.

One of them shouted, "Drop the gun! Right now!"

Joshua peed his pants. Then he dropped his toy in the gravel.

Three officers rushed him. They pushed him onto the hood of a cruiser and roughly patted him down. Of course, once they picked up the gun Joshua had dropped, they knew it for a toy. They gave Joshua a lecture about disguising toys as weapons, much like the lectures he'd already heard from his dad and me. Then they let him go.

As I worked at pulling this information from my frantic son that afternoon, he continued to curse the police for confiscating the toy gun.

"I'm going to sue those bastards!" he bawled. "They stole my gun! That's illegal!"

When he eventually calmed down, he was able to appreciate the officers for their restraint. He even acknowledged the wisdom of his dad and me for having predicted such an event.

"From now on, I'm going to do everything you tell me," he said.

After Benn told me of Joshua's arrest in the cemetery, I drove to the police department and used the lobby phone to contact the arresting officer.

While I waited for him to come off patrol, my cell phone rang. It was Joshua, making use of his one phone call.

"You've got to get me out of here," he said. "I cannot stay here."

"Honey, I'll do the best I can."

"They took my screwdriver."

"What were you doing with a screwdriver?"

"I didn't do anything! I was just poking around the cemetery."

"With a screwdriver?"

"It doesn't matter. Just get me out of here. I'm telling you: I cannot be here. They won't give me my meds."

"I can't promise I'll be able to get you out tonight. I have to find out how much the bail is."

"They told me. It's six hundred dollars."

"Joshua, listen," I said, trying to keep my voice calm and reassuring, "I don't think I can get that much out of the bank machine. But I will get it tomorrow as soon as the bank opens. Understand? So, for now, I want you to be polite, no matter what they say to you. Okay?"

"Just get me out. I have to go now."

While I waited for the patrolman to meet me in the lobby, I tried to picture my son locked in a place where I couldn't reach or protect him. Because Joshua was over eighteen by this time, he was lodged with adults in the county jail. Protecting Joshua had been my role for so long, I didn't know how else to respond to his poor choices. More than once, I've gotten between Joshua and the police. One time, an officer wanted to question him privately about a restaurant break-in; I refused to leave the room.

"You can't protect him all his life," the officer said.

"Joshua has a congenital brain disorder," I informed him, lowering the pitch of my voice so as not to cry. "I have a binder this thick"—I spread my thumb and index finger four inches—"filled with his medical records. I'd be glad to show them to you."

The officer sighed and proceeded to question Joshua in my presence. But he was right: I couldn't protect Joshua forever.

The policeman who'd arrested Joshua was Officer Wells. He entered the lobby of the police department where I'd been waiting and sat beside me on a bench. He didn't look much older than my son. When he spoke, his voice took on the quieting tones of a minister comforting the bereaved.

"Joshua was very cooperative when I questioned him in the cemetery," the young officer told me. "But I still had to charge him with attempted burglary and possession of burglary tools."

"Burglary tools? You mean the screwdriver?" I said. "What's he supposed to have burgled?"

"A witness saw him trying to break into the tool shed. He worked on the padlock for at least ten minutes, but he couldn't get it open."

"He likes locks," I said. "He always has. But he wouldn't steal."

Officer Wells gave me the number of the county jail, so I could inform the staff about Joshua's mental health issues.

Rich and I hired a lawyer to represent Joshua at his arraignment the following afternoon. Joshua was led into the courtroom in handcuffs and orange jumpsuit. He appeared calm, in control of himself.

He responded politely to the judge's questions and did what his lawyer told him. He was released to us a few minutes later.

Joshua wanted to plead not guilty and go to trial.

"That wouldn't be a good idea," the lawyer told us when we met with him in his office the next week.

Rich and I sat across from the attorney at a gleaming mahogany table. Joshua, refusing to sit with us, stood instead against a bookcase filled with thick volumes the same mahogany color as the table.

"I didn't do anything illegal," Joshua responded belligerently. "I like antique locks. The lock on that door was the kind I like to study. That cop had no reason to haul my ass to jail."

"Look, Joshua, the law doesn't care what you intended. The judge isn't going to try to read your mind. You were in the cemetery. There's a witness. She will testify that she saw you trying to break open the door."

"That's bullshit! I have every right to be in the cemetery. It's public property."

"If you go to trial, the chance that you'll be found guilty is very high. Do you want to spend several months in jail?"

I kept waiting for the lawyer to give up trying to reason with Joshua. Arguing, I've learned, doesn't work with a kid who inhabits his own peculiar reality. But

Joshua finally agreed to plead no contest. The judge sentenced him to three months' probation and forty hours of community service, and told him to stay out of the cemetery.

Joshua, now twenty-one, needs far less protecting than he once did, because, for all his bluster, he did somehow incorporate the lessons he received from his trauma-tinged encounters with the police. From Maddy he learned to stay away from fire. From Officer Holstrum he learned to hang out with a higher caliber of friends. After the toy gun incident, he surrendered his craving to own a weapon. And after his arrest, he decided to avoid situations that might make him look suspicious to others.

All of those are lessons Rich and I have tried to teach him. But Joshua' s learning curve requires drama sufficient to cut through his compulsions—a form of parenting that was never in our power to give but that, on at least a few occasions, has been helpfully facilitated by law enforcement.

—*Caren Hathaway Caldwell*

Something in Common

A famous quote, by Elizabeth Stone, says that having a child is like having your heart walking outside of your body. I think that's absolutely true. But for me, having a child is also like having a walking, talking ulcer.

I've inherited my Ukrainian grandmother's impressive worrying abilities, which bypassed my mother and hit me with double the anxiety. Or maybe it's because I'm a single mom and I have to worry enough for two people. At any rate, I named my heart—and ulcer—Tommy.

While pregnant with my son, I worried about everything from what I was eating to potential complications. To soothe myself, I envisioned a mellow, dark-haired, dark-eyed little boy who loved to read and looked just like my bookwormish self.

I had no idea that prenatal anxiety would be a piece of cake compared to parental anxiety, which began the day Tommy was born and just escalated from that point on. When he started first grade, I really started to worry—about everything from grades to friends to what he was eating at lunch. Suddenly, there were whole aspects of his life that were unknown to me. Tommy had been in daycare since he was an infant, and it had always been meticulously planned, but now I could barely remember if it was gym or library day.

To complicate matters, although Tommy is a talkative kid, if things aren't going well, he sometimes clams up. So the easiest way for me to determine how he's doing at school (besides bothering his teacher with a daily e-mail) is by sitting down with him when he does his homework.

It was at the dining room table that I discovered one of those quiet little joys of motherhood. Tommy and I hold our pencils in the same unusual way; on the fourth finger (the ring finger) of our right hands, rather than the middle finger. That small similarity put a smile on my face for the rest of the evening.

It was also at that table that I discovered a huge difference between us. Though my little guy loves when I read him a good book, he's really not into the reading himself. In fact, reading is much more of a struggle for Tommy than I could ever have expected it to be. I'd always thought reading would just "click" for my son. Instead, a lot of sighing and whining comes along with any reading assignment. I'd had high hopes that Tommy would be able to pick up a book and lose himself in the pages—to wash ashore on a desert island, to find himself in Hogwart's ramparts, or to scale Mount Everest's icy rocks. But as our struggle with simple reading assignments increased, I began to really worry about his lack of comprehension.

One night, a few months after first grade started, we struggled over his newest assignment: phonics. Our task was to pick out the short *e* sound in words. Tommy was grumbling about it, kicking the table, and muttering that reading was "too hard."

"Let's try it together, how about that?" I asked. "Can you read me a word?"

"Feet."

"Is that a short *e* or a long *e*?"

He put his head in his hands. "I don't know."

"Honey, you have to at least try."

He sighed. "Feet."

"Short *e*?"

"I don't know. This is too hard."

"It's a short *e*," I said. Then I thought about it. "No, I think it's a long *e*."

Tommy looked at me with renewed interest.

"Feet. Feeeeeet. Feet. Feeeeet," I experimented.

"Mommy?"

I looked at the paper. "Met. Meet."

"Mommy?"

"Shhh, sweetie. Met. Meet. Feet. Feeeet."

"Mom? Is it a short *e*?"

I felt for a moment as if I had fallen down the rabbit hole. "I think it's a long *e*."

"Are you sure?"

"No."

"You're not?" Tommy looked absolutely bewildered at my revelation.

I couldn't blame him. And the more I thought about it, the more bewildered I got. Language was one thing that had never failed me, but it was certainly failing me then. Even worse, it was first-grade phonics. Twenty-eight years old, and I wasn't sure whether "feet" was a short *e* or a long *e*.

"What do you think?" I asked Tommy.

"I don't know." He looked at me, blue eyes searching my face. "How come you don't know?"

"I don't know why I don't know."

At that pronouncement, his eyes widened in shock and his forehead wrinkled like a seventy-year-old man's.

"Now what?" he asked.

Good question, I thought. So I did what I always do when I need advice: I called my mom.

Fortunately, Mom is able to distinguish between a long *e* and a short *e*. She patiently explained the difference, and a few seconds after her explanation, I was confused all over again. This went on for a while, until we decided that maybe it would be easier for her to just explain it to Tommy. I handed him the phone.

After I put my son to bed, I tried to figure out what was more disturbing: that I couldn't help my son or that I didn't understand phonics. Being unable to understand something basic was worrisome, but even more disturbing was that I wasn't able to help Tommy when he needed it. I expected problems with algebra or physics later, but phonics in first grade? No way.

A few nights later, my mom, my dad, Tommy, and I went out to dinner. As we waited outside in the unseasonably warm October air for a table to open up, I brought up the phone debacle to Mom. "I feel like an idiot. Why didn't I know that?"

She smiled. "You still don't get it?"

"Get what? Phonics?"

"Yeah, you still don't get it?"

"Obviously not." I shook my head. "It doesn't make any sense to me."

"I'm not surprised."

"No?"

Mom put a hand on my arm. "You honestly don't remember? You were tutored the entire summer between first and second grade for phonics."

"Oh yeah, now that you mention it. My tutor had dark hair, used to be a teacher, and had a son—"

"Who was a preemie, so she stayed home after he was born. She tutored you in phonics because you were miserable at it. Then, at the end of the summer, she went on vacation for a week and you lost everything. She came back and had to start from scratch with you."

"So what happened?"

"She quit."

"Oh, great. That's reassuring," I said.

"I'm serious. You couldn't do phonics to save your life. Never had any comprehension of it. But you could read."

"Without phonics?"

"That was the funny thing." Mom paused as a large group of people walked around us. "Phonics was supposed to teach you how to read. But you already could. In first grade you were reading at a fifth-grade level. I remember you came home from school angry because they would only let you pick out books that were 'for babies.'"

"Weird."

"That's what the tutor thought, too. She didn't think you could comprehend it at all, but somehow you'd compensated for that."

"Huh." I looked over at Tommy, who was sitting on my dad's lap and pointing out the intricacies of Super Mario Brothers on his Nintendo DS to my dad. "So what do I do about Tommy?"

"What do you mean?"

"I don't get it, Mom. Honestly, not at all. How am I supposed to help him when I don't understand it?" I made a sound somewhere between a growl and a sigh in my throat. "I wish there was someone else to help him with this."

"You'll get through it. And you have plenty of people to help you."

"And what if he doesn't get it? What if he has the same problem I had—that I have?"

"He'll get through it, too. Have you talked to his teacher?"

"On the phone. We have a parent-teacher conference scheduled for next week."

"Talk to her. Maybe he just needs extra help."

I wish I had my mother's confidence, but I couldn't help worrying that I just didn't know enough. After all, I'm still discovering the similarities between

Tommy and me, like the way we hold our pens and our love of science fiction.

I'm still discovering our differences, too, like his athletic nature and outgoing personality versus my inherent shyness and bookish nature. I've done things I never thought I'd enjoy doing, from picking up bugs to finding some fun in math. Life is a little more exciting and a little less predictable with Tommy. Up until that point, the differences were things I'd expected or was excited at discovering.

But the issue with reading was something I didn't expect and felt anxious, rather than excited, about. Perhaps the two of us do have a similar processing problem with phonics and sounds. But if that's the case, the consequences of it are not the same. I learned to read and love to read despite it; Tommy's struggling to read and dislikes reading because of it.

Maybe it's the differences between our personalities and childhood experiences that allowed for my compensation and for my son's struggle with phonics and reading. I was a shy, quiet, and solitary child. My grandmother watched me during the day while my parents worked, and there were no kids in my neighborhood to play with. It's no wonder I learned to read at an early age; reading was my escape, my recreation. It still is.

But Thomas is more active; he goes to daycare and has a ton of friends. He was social from the get-go and would rather be in perpetual motion than slow down and read. If my personality and childhood had been more like his, maybe I'd have struggled with reading, too. If his personality and situation were more like mine, maybe he'd be reading now.

After we got home that warm October evening, Tommy ran into the garage. He told me he had something to do before he went to bed. It would just take a minute, he promised, and he wasn't going to get into any trouble. Three minutes later, he called me to come out to the garage to look at something.

We have a two-car garage but only one car. In the empty spot, Tommy had taken blue chalk and written on the cement. I knelt next to him to see the words better: *blow and gene ar my fabet culrs.*

"Blue and green are my favorite colors," he pronounced slowly and deliberately as he pointed to each word. He turned to me and smiled.

I smiled back and hugged him. As I held his skinny little body close, I realized something: it was the first time he'd attempted to write something on his own, without begging me to spell for him as he wrote.

Months later, after many tests and meetings with his teachers, guidance counselors, a pediatrician, and a school psychologist, we discovered that Tommy's reading problems stemmed from a quirk: "attention deficit hyperactivity disorder, primarily inattentive." A quirk, it turns out, we happen to share; it just manifested differently in Tommy. My whole life I've been flighty, unable to concentrate, my mind always a million miles away. I'd seen it in my son, but because it was normal for me, I'd assumed it was normal for everyone.

After Tommy's ADHD diagnosis, I thought things would clear up and life would get easier. In some ways it has, but challenges remain. His pediatrician prescribed Focalin, a drug that helps him concentrate, and he is in a Title I program in his school, getting extra help with reading. He's still struggling, though, and I am in close contact with his school as we decide which steps to take next.

That I, an avid reader and writer, have a son who is struggling to do what I love so much might seem ironic to some. In a way, though, it makes perfect sense. Knowing what it's like to struggle in school has helped me to understand my son better and to be more compassionate toward him. When Tommy struggles, I don't get frustrated, wondering why he can't just work it through, and reprimand him. Instead, I remember my own frustration when I was in school and we try something different. Whereas I was the child in school who was always staring out the windows and getting in trouble for not paying attention, my son is getting help instead of getting yelled at. Though progress is hard-won and slow-going, we've had resources I never imagined and received support from people who care deeply about giving my son the best opportunities in life.

Of course, the impressive worrying abilities I inherited from my Ukrainian grandmother still prod and poke me, keeping me up at night, making me wonder about all the things I can't control. And some things are not within anyone's control. Medication can only go so far with ADHD, and we have to constantly find and test out other ways of teaching him to see what works best. But I have become more comfortable with the gray areas of life and have more faith that it will all work out in the end. I've also learned to rejoice in things I might otherwise have taken for granted. Every night that Tommy reads better than the previous one is a victory; every sign he reads on the street is a cause for celebration; and every note he leaves me, regardless of misspellings, is a treasure.

—Leesa Gehman

Then a Hero Comes Along

My son was born fighting for his life. According to the fetal monitor, the forty hours of nonproductive labor had taken its toll. Jonathan's heart rate was dropping. My unborn baby was dying. Every second became precious as I was raced to the operating room for an emergency cesarean section. The surgery was a success. A few days later, the hospital allowed us to take our healthy baby home.

Nothing seemed abnormal in Jonathan's development until he turned two; then we began to worry. His speech was garbled. He had difficulty putting three words together. His fine motor skills, such as manipulating puzzle pieces, were nonexistent. More disturbing, Jonathan began having grand mal seizures. We saw several different neurologists and had numerous tests and several CT scans performed, but the results were always the same—there was nothing irregular about our son's brain.

Determined our child wouldn't be left behind his peers, my husband John and I spent several hours a week working with Jonathan—reading, crafting, dancing to simple rhythms. But our efforts were in vain. He couldn't draw the simplest of shapes, and his speech was still halting and garbled. My confidence and patience spent, I agreed with John to have our son tested by the local university.

Their findings devastated us. During the meeting, we heard phrases such as "developmentally delayed" and "speech impairment."

I closed my eyes and sank deeper into the chair, trying to wrap my brain around what the evaluators were saying. I'd had such big dreams for Jonathan. He'd be the star on the school football team, sing solos in the choir, give the valedictory address at his high school graduation. Now, these impersonal people were telling me my child would do well to use scissors or to even speak well enough that others could understand him.

"What are you saying," I asked, "that he's retarded?"

"No," one evaluator said. "He's just delayed."

Just delayed? The diagnosis did little to ease my anxiety. How would other children, who could do what he couldn't, accept Jonathan?

We knew that the sooner we received occupational and speech therapy for Jonathan, the better his chances were for overcoming his obstacles. A few months later, we enrolled him in the local preschool. The teachers specialized in special education, and despite daily tears when I dropped him off, Jonathan flourished. By the end of the year, he could color within the lines, skip, and read simple nursery rhymes.

Jonathan had been born fighting for his life, but in elementary school, he fought to fit in. His verbal skills improved, thanks to the speech program in the school district, but some of the same children who had played with him in preschool now tortured and isolated him because he was "different."

Some school days were rougher than others. Jonathan would come home in tears, upset because a classmate ridiculed his speech problem or his lack of coordination. My heart broke with his. It outraged me to learn that some classroom parent volunteers were behaving in the same insensitive way toward my son.

In fourth grade, a classmate was instructed by his mother to end his friendship with Jonathan. Her reason? Jonathan was "different" and being associated with him would only harm Rodney's chances for success in school. A few days later, the same woman added insult to injury by refusing Jonathan a cupcake at the class party. "It's only for the 'normal' students," she sneered as she walked past.

I squirmed angrily in my seat at the kitchen table, pounding my fist against my leg, as Jonathan relayed the story to me that afternoon. *Just what did she perceive as "normal"? Certainly not her actions toward my child,* I thought. I imagined grabbing the woman by the hair, slamming her onto the floor, and grinding her face into the kitchen linoleum. "Just wait till I meet her. She'll rather have been in a fistfight with a windmill after I'm through with her. I'll—"

Jonathan frowned and shook his head. "Mama, please. You can't fight my battles for me. Besides, that woman needs our prayers, not our punches."

He was right. Confronting the woman would accomplish nothing; in fact, it would only make matters worse. "When did you get so smart?" I mumbled.

"Simple. You and Daddy are always telling me to pray for people who hurt me," he replied, then walked outside to play. I was grateful he'd listened to a few things I'd told him.

For the rest of the school year, Jonathan began to let his inner beauty blossom by using respect and manners and by showing compassion for those who needed it. As a result, his actions influenced some of the toughest kids in the class, and they too began modeling positive behavior. His teachers as well as his dad and I were delighted.

A few years earlier, I'd been in a near-fatal car accident, resulting in nerve damage in my right arm. Unable to work, I passed my time by writing and submitting stories to different publications. When Jonathan was in fifth grade, we were both overjoyed when an essay of mine was accepted for an anthology of a well-known book series. He became my biggest fan, telling everyone he knew what I'd accomplished and that I was his hero.

It warmed my heart that my son thought so highly of me. But "hero" wasn't a word I'd use to describe myself.

I was leery when, at the end of his fifth-grade year, Jonathan joined 4H. If kids his own age treated him so badly, surely the teasing by the older children in 4H would be much worse. I believed his joining was a recipe for disaster. But I was wrong. Jonathan was treated with respect, and he was nurtured and encouraged by the older kids. As a result, his self-confidence grew. After only a month, he announced plans to compete in a 4H speech contest. My heart fell. Jonathan still stuttered, and it worsened when he spoke in public.

"I can do this, Mama," he said when I questioned his decision.

Every day after school, we practiced his speech, and each time he stumbled terribly on the simplest of words.

"Again. I wanna try it again," he'd demand through gritted teeth.

His determination and all that practice paid off. Jonathan dominated the district-level contest, securing a third-place ribbon and advancing to the regional level. Regional, where there would be more people and the competition was twice as hard. Again, my heart sank.

We had only a month to practice, and with dogged determination, Jonathan went over and over his speech. It became a common sight at sunset to see him sitting on the slide in the backyard, delivering his speech to his younger brother and the dog.

During those times, I'd stand at the kitchen window watching. Bowing my head in prayer, I'd ask God not only for my boy to win but for the confidence he needed.

Time passed all too quickly and soon the contest day arrived.

Jonathan wasn't concerned. "I can say this speech in my sleep," he boasted as we drove to the school where the contest would be held.

His bravado ebbed like water through a sieve as we walked into the auditorium. He balked at the door when he saw the sea of participants milling around the room. "I can't do this," he moaned. "I feel ill; take me home."

"You'll do wonderful," I said, smiling as I put my arm around his shoulders. "When you speak, you'll find your strength in here," I continued, pointing to his heart, "and the knowledge in here," I finished, dropping a kiss on his head. I wished him luck, entered the room with his daddy, and found a seat.

I was thankful Jonathan couldn't hear the speeches before his. They were good, very good. He'd definitely have his work cut out for him.

At last his turn arrived. He entered the room, as straight and proud as a tin soldier, confidence shining in his slate-blue eyes. In an unfaltering, clear voice, he delivered his speech, and then, with the confidence of a politician, he fielded all the judges' questions.

The wait for the judges' decisions was worse than a trip to the dentist. Pacing nervously, Jonathan checked the auditorium window every five minutes for the results. Finally, they were posted. Wading through a mixture of jubilant and morose participants, we made our way to the window and scanned over the list. There, in third place, was Jonathan.

"Thank you, God!" Jonathan cried, dropping to his knees. At the awards assembly, he fairly floated as he walked across the stage to accept his prize.

That night, when I tucked Jonathan into bed, I saw the beloved white ribbon clutched in his hand. A smile of pure happiness remained on his lips as he slept. Tenderly, I kissed him on the cheek, and gently removing the ribbon from his sweaty grasp, I tacked the newly won prize on Jonathan's bulletin board.

Standing in the doorway, I stared at my slumbering son. Before my eyes, he was growing from a chubby-faced boy into a handsome young man. A lump formed in my throat as I thought of all the things he'd overcome—speech and developmental delays, stuttering, bullying—and his determination to overcome all those obstacles. Looking at my courageous son, I remembered the day my story had been published and he'd told me I was his hero.

On tiptoe, I crossed the room and gave him a final kiss on the cheek. "No, Jonathan," I whispered, "you're my hero." And he is.

—Debbie Roppolo

A Tale of Two Brothers

On that cold morning in our Northern California town, I tapped lightly on my son Andy's door to wake him for an early flight back to the East Coast, where he is a freshman in college.

During his three-week winter break, though he'd been perfectly pleasant, he was always in a hurry to be anywhere but home, and my husband and I were struck by how little time he needed to spend with us.

"Have you had a meaningful conversation with him?" I asked my husband after a week and a half. "I sure haven't."

"No," he sighed, "but he's thrown me a few lines."

Paranoid that we had gone wrong somewhere along the way, we'd polled our friends in similar circumstances, and they'd assured us that his behavior was normal. "Join the club," they'd laughed. So we'd relaxed and made ourselves available for conversation and meals and were grateful for the scraps that came our way.

It was clear, however, that Andy couldn't wait to get back to school, so much so that I was ready for him to leave.

Just as I took a quick swig of coffee before we had to leave for the airport, Andy stepped out fully dressed, packed and ready to go. The night before, he had printed out his boarding pass and arranged for a ride from JFK airport to his school in Connecticut. Amazing.

It had been quite a different scene one week earlier when Andy's twenty-year-old brother Matthew, who has autism, prepared for his trip back to Pennsylvania, where he attends a special school.

"Mom," he'd said the night before his trip, "I need to make pancakes in the morning."

His flight was at 7:10 A.M.

"Of course," I said.

It was an outrageous request, but one I'd anticipated. Travel days were hard for Matthew, and sticking to his routine would increase the odds of the day being a successful one. So we were up at 4:15 A.M., setting his place at the table and warming the griddle. After breakfast, he counted the money he had earned during the break doing garden work and left it piled neatly in the drawer next to his bed. It was no use telling him to put it in a wallet or in the bank.

"I like the dollars stacked," he said, "and we're not going to talk about it anymore."

I looked to see if he had cut his bangs the night before, another one of his pre-travel rituals.

Oh, man, he sure had.

Matthew is high functioning but socially inept, and it's necessary for him to fly with a helper. This time, he would be flying back to school with a young woman who worked at his school. She had flown Matthew home and had been touring California during his stay.

Sending Matthew to a residential school was the last thing that my husband and I thought we would ever do. While painfully aware of his disability, Matthew has always wanted to be a regular guy attending a regular school. But just a few days into his fifteenth year, he decided that he should drive a car like a regular guy and drove mine through the front wall in our garage.

There were other unsettling episodes. One day during his freshman year at our local high school, he observed a guy pushing his girlfriend flirtatiously and then tapping her on the head. After Matthew tried the same move on her friend with a little too much force, I was summoned to his school and found him crying in the principal's office.

"Joe did it to Sue, and she liked it!" he sobbed.

Just when we thought things were calming down from the incident at school, a letter arrived from an attorney asking us to contact him about a bicycle accident involving Matthew. It turned out that a month before, while riding his bike, Matthew had run into a young boy on his bike.

"Matthew? What's this about a bike accident?"

"Who told you?"

"Someone sent me a letter. Was the boy you bumped into hurt?"

"Pretty much."

Dear God.

"Was he bleeding?"

"Probably. Am I in trouble?"

It became clear that Matthew's impulsive actions were putting others in danger and that it was no longer safe for him to live in the community in which he'd grown up. He needed more supervision, more than we or the local school could provide. It seemed unfathomable to me that, after all of the years of struggling through school meetings, countless hours of therapy, and repeated damage control with neighbors, it had come to this. I felt incredibly sad and defeated, but I was too exhausted to keep fighting.

So the search for a residential facility began, and we were lucky to find a great one, Camphill Special School near Philadelphia. There, Matthew learned that he had a purpose, and he was an important part of the community of disabled people with whom he lived.

During visits home, Matthew, a self-proclaimed landscape specialist, is obsessed with garden work—mowing, blowing, and edging with precision, and when he is not doing it himself, he studies other garden crews in our neighborhood and around town. They all know him and are kind to him, as are the neighbors for whom they work.

This year, after three or four days, he grew tired of gardening and announced that he was ready to hang out with his friends. The only problem is he has no friends.

"You can go to the movies with me and my friends," Andy offered as he always does, but Matthew refused.

"I have my own friends," he said proudly and proceeded to call people who had been kind to him five years ago during his first and only year in public high school.

He called them over and over and over. Their mothers took most of the calls, and I'm sure they wondered why I didn't put a stop to his obsessive behavior.

"Matthew," I said, "calling once or twice is fine, but if you keep calling, that's bothering, and you'll make people angry." I told him that when I was his age, a guy I liked called me too much and it drove me away.

"But did you still think he was nice?" Matthew asked, his lip quivering.

Before I could answer, the sound of a lawnmower around the corner distracted him, and with the promise of a friendly garden crew, he was off with a grin. I could exhale for the moment, but I remained constantly on edge until delivering him into the hands of his travel companion for his flight back to school.

"Having a brother like Matthew will make Andy a better person," well-meaning friends had said when Matthew was first diagnosed with autism at age three. Although their words were meant to comfort and encourage me, they implied that tough times were ahead for baby Andy, which strengthened my resolve to protect him.

Andy was five when I first noticed playmates in the park teasing him about his brother's hand-flapping, and I flew to his side, ready to take on the little jerks.

"He has a brain problem," Andy was explaining to them cheerfully. "He can't help it."

The boys nodded anxiously and backed away.

"Andy," I said with a lump in my throat, "I'm so proud of you. That was very loyal."

"Thank you," he said. "I'm proud of you, too."

It wasn't long, though, before the novelty of educating his peers wore off. By the time Andy was seven, his exuberant explanations had turned defensive, and I would swoop in with suggestions of snappy comeback lines for him to use in a pinch: "Takes one to know one!" "Whatever!" And Andy's favorite, "Get a life!"

But when he was twelve and entering middle school, Andy had tired of coming up with clever retorts as Matthew's impulsive behavior and public meltdowns increased. He stopped having friends over and started refusing invitations.

"The last time I went to a friend's house," he said, "they asked me why we never hang out at my house. I don't want to say 'because I'm tired of apologizing for my brother.'"

"Would you like to talk to someone?" I asked. "Or maybe join some kind of a sibling support group?"

"Could I just talk to you sometimes?" he replied quietly. "And sometimes can we do stuff without Matthew—just you and me?"

"Of course!" I said, choking up. "How about tomorrow?"

Wouldn't you know it, the next day Andy had a slight fever, but we decided he was well enough to go to nearby San Francisco for the day, anyway.

The next few years with Matthew were especially hard, for him and for our family. Andy prided himself on being one of the few people who could calm Matthew down when he was upset and on being the one who could make Matthew laugh the hardest.

"I've got him," he would say when Matthew would climb off the yellow school bus in tears. The two would go out to the mulberry tree in the back yard and sit on opposite branches until Andy got Matthew to smile. When they'd walk back into the house, Andy would flash me a secret victorious smile, and I would put my hand over my heart in reply.

When I was having doubts about whether to send Matthew to a residential school, I overheard Andy telling my husband that he'd miss Matthew.

"But at least Mom won't be so worried all of the time."

A month to the day after Matthew first left for his school in Pennsylvania, Andy, who was then in ninth grade, burst into the house after school, looking nervous but exhilarated. He asked if I could help him clean up the house—now.

"Luke and Greg are on their way over!"

I couldn't even remember the last time he'd had friends over.

Within minutes, the clutter of the house was stacked on my bed, the house was vacuumed, and the toilets were cleaned. I was shoving the mop back in the closet when the doorbell rang.

"Hi, guys," I said, grinning like a modern June Cleaver. "He's back in his room."

Before I could bake the cookies that I had thrown together in my manic state, the boys rushed out of Andy's room and announced they were walking downtown. They flew out the front door laughing, and I burst into tears.

When Andy was born, I still thought Matthew was just a regular two-year-old. My only worry was whether I could ever love this second baby as much as I did the first, and the feeling evaporated the moment I was alone with Andy for the first time in my hospital room, kissing his fuzzy baby head and studying his chubby hands.

Now, I had two sons—brothers—and I imagined them growing up together. Andy would look up to Matthew and learn from him. When they were in school, the teachers would say, "Oh, you're Matthew Shumaker's brother!" and Andy would beam. They would drive around together as teenagers, have the same friends, and I would raise them to be loyal to one another. They might go to different colleges; that would be healthy. But wouldn't it be great if they lived near each other as men and if their wives were friends?

I could never have known then that Andy and Matthew would blossom at about the same time—3,000 miles apart.

I couldn't have imagined that Matthew would be a young man with autism, and that I'd be grateful that he was living and learning with teachers who understood him and valued him.

And I could never have guessed that Andy, after suffering through his reclusive period, would experience a joyous rebirth as he entered high school and that he would reclaim the class-clown status that he'd left behind in grammar school. I wouldn't have predicted that he would enjoy sports, friends, and classes, and that by senior year, his homebody stage would be a distant memory as he made plans to go to college on the East Coast. But I would not have been surprised that he'd be a National Merit Scholar, that he'd get into Yale, and that we'd joke that it was all because he had a good mother.

When I drove Andy to the airport after winter break, he asked me if I had heard Matthew speak Spanish.

"No. He speaks Spanish?"

"He pretends to speak Spanish," Andy said with a smile, "when he hangs out with some of the garden crews."

"Oh no, that's terrible!" I said. "They must think he's racist or something!"

"Come on, Mom," he laughed. "They think it's hilarious. They can tell he's . . . you know."

Andy jumped out of the car, dragging his huge duffle bag behind him.

"I love you, Mom. Thanks for everything," he said. "Don't worry so much about Matthew. He'll find his way. And you know I'll always look out for him."

He walked into the airport, and I drove away, conscious that my eighteen-year-old son had just thrown me a line. But I also knew he meant it. And I grabbed it gratefully.

—*Laura Shumaker*

Thank You for This Boy, Amen

As we walked up the broad steps of our church, Nancy glanced up at me and hesitated. "What's the matter, Mommy, you look sad."

I smiled down at my seven-year-old, not surprised that this intuitive and sensitive child sensed my mood. "Oh, nothing, honey," I said. "I just feel a little nervous for Kevin."

Actually, I felt a sick lump in my stomach and wished this night were over.

My thirteen-year-old son Christopher and my husband Roger had already found seats for us in one of the front pews so we would be able to see Kevin clearly. Parishioners quickly filled the seats, eager to participate in the Lenten Holy Thursday services. Members of the senior Catholic Youth Organization (CYO) would each read a passage from the Bible, one for each station of the cross in remembrance of

Christ's suffering. Kevin's reading was for the twelfth station of the cross, when Christ dies. Socially immature and with few friends, Kevin had at last found a small niche within the CYO group, which was led by an understanding and compassionate priest. Kev had been thrilled to invite many family friends and neighbors to join us for the service.

I was proud but upset that Kevin had volunteered for an activity that I felt certain would be difficult for him and might well embarrass him. It wouldn't be the first time. His childhood had been filled with emotional pain. Severe learning disabilities, a speech impediment, and social awkwardness made each day of school a trial for him. With his chronic asthma and poor coordination, he was considered a klutz by peers, who didn't include him in sports, games, or playground and after-school activities. Many of his classmates, misjudging Kev's learning disabilities and stuttering for a lack of intelligence, labeled him a "retard." Now sixteen and a junior in high school, Kevin had learned to control his stuttering much of the time. He had made progress academically, but his speech still became unintelligible when he was nervous or upset, and so he continued to see a speech therapist once a week at school.

Despite these challenges, Kevin possessed a joy and zest for life that I envied. We had adopted Kevin and brought him home when he was only a week old. Roger and I loved him like crazy and helped him in every way we could, but neither of us possessed Kevin's inherent nonjudgmental personality and positive attitude. His unrelenting optimism helped him to cope and to compensate for the problems he faced daily. He was accepting and tolerant of others, and considered everyone he met to be a friend. Through the years, I've often wished I could meet his birth parents so that I could discover which of them (or perhaps both) enjoyed the joyous spirit they had passed on to our child.

Now, tonight, he was going to stand up in front of hundreds of people and recite the story of his savior's ultimate sacrifice.

The buzz of conversation quieted as Monsignor walked to the podium and greeted us warmly. He spoke softly, gently reminding us of what Christ had endured for us. The lights in the church clicked off, leaving only the light over the lectern glowing on the Bible. One by one, the CYO members, dressed in simple white robes, solemnly shared their readings. Some were nervous and read so quickly that it was hard to understand them. Others, composed and confident, read slowly and deliberately. Finally, it was Kevin's turn.

He smiled as he opened the Bible to the passage he had practiced reading endlessly at home over the last few weeks. My husband's hand closed over mine. Chris and Nancy looked at me for reassurance I was unable to provide.

"The . . . the . . . the . . ." Kevin began. He stopped. His mouth twisted slowly as he tried painfully to say the next word. Nothing. He wasn't stuttering; he was blocked, unable to speak.

We sat paralyzed in the quiet stillness. I looked away from Kevin and tried not to cry. My family stared straight ahead. None of us could look at each other. Then, as we all waited in the dark, soundless church, I felt a tiny warm glow begin to flicker inside of me. It grew slowly, until I felt consumed by its radiance. Moments later, I realized it had to be the prayers of everyone in the church, forming a slow, single wave of hope directed toward Kevin, willing him to speak.

"Lord spoke." Two more words.

Again, his mouth contorted painfully. He took a deep breath—a breath from which he seemed to draw strength from parishioners, family, and friends. Then, he continued his reading, halting for endless minutes between many words. A smile crept into his eyes and over his face as he slowly and deliberately read the exceptionally long passage. Finally, he finished and just stood there a moment. Then he grinned unabashedly, gave a slight wave, and stepped down from the lectern.

I had to grab Chris' hands to stop him from applauding, and Nancy gave me a big hug. There were two more passages to be read. Afterward, as the church lights clicked on one by one, it seemed as if I had been on a long journey and was now returning to reality. My family sat silently for a while, each us saying thank you in our own way before going into the church hall to share refreshments with our church community.

I thought I might find Kevin upset or embarrassed, but I should have known better. God's wonderful gifts of optimism and joy hadn't let him down. He stood in the center of a large group, grinning broadly as compliment after compliment was bestowed upon him.

"That was great, Kev. We all felt Jesus' pain when you were trying to speak."

"Congratulations on a great job. You really hung in there. I would have flipped out."

"Did you feel our prayers as we struggled with you?"

"You really have guts."

Kevin laughed as more CYO members gathered around him, gently joshing and teasing. He was part of a group—and loving it!

Father Charles, the CYO moderator, hugged Kevin tightly. "Well, Kevin. You are our hero tonight. I'm so proud of you. Every person here certainly could imagine the physical agony and mental suffering of Jesus when He hung on the cross as we watched you struggle. Your pain certainly showed how the Lord suffered before he died. You gave new meaning to the word 'courage.'"

After the group drifted away, Kevin joined us for cake and punch.

"Hey, Mom. I told you not to worry. I knew I could do it. At first, I really got upset when I got stuck. But then I remembered what my speech therapist tells me every week. 'Kev,' she says, 'when you have something to say and people care about you, they'll wait until you can finish.' She was right. Isn't that great?"

"Yes, it is," I said, smiling, as I began my own silent prayer. *God is great, God is good . . .*

—*Gerry Di Gesu*

Hearing Hope

They put her in a little box, a kind of aquarium for babies—a little room raised about three feet off the floor. The front wall was glass, a six-by-eight foot rectangle that allowed us to watch our baby take the test that none of us could have studied for.

Meagan, our two-year-old daughter, was the fishie in that bowl. Her mother, Laural, her four-year-old sister, Heather, and I watched her through the imposing glass wall. The glass was such that Meagan couldn't see us. She was alone, as far as she knew, and she looked bewildered and afraid. She chewed on her hand as she searched the room with her eyes.

Our precious toddler had been put in that box to determine if she could hear. Months before, Laural had begun to fear that something was amiss, but she couldn't rationalize her fear. Meagan was an incredibly bright child, and developmentally, she had kept pace with her older sister. Heather had walked at eight months, Meagan at eleven; both girls could dress themselves at eighteen months, and both of them were potty trained before their second birthdays. According to our pediatrician, Meagan had reached every developmental checkpoint on or ahead of schedule. By all accounts, Meagan was a healthy, normal toddler.

Except she didn't talk.

Meagan made lots of noises. She laughed and cried, and she made incredibly delightful sounds, but she didn't speak. If she wanted something, she asked for it by pointing. Time and again she'd grab my finger and pull me to the kitchen, where she's jab her finger excitedly at the cabinet where her mother kept the saltine crackers. She'd laugh and jump and point until she was rewarded with a cracker. She'd hold her prize high above her head and call it by some adorable nonsense word that toddlers tend to invent until they learn the proper names of things. A cracker for Meagan meant a kiss for Dad. I was always happy to oblige Meagan on our excursions to the kitchen.

Our pediatrician told us there was nothing to worry about. Some kids just developed speech later than others, he said.

Months passed, and Meagan still didn't develop speech. Then one day her mother observed her pressing her ear on the canister of a running vacuum cleaner. She immediately scheduled a visit with our family doctor.

Our pediatrician performed rudimentary tests on Meagan. Essentially, he made noises behind her back and watched her closely for reactions. The results were inconclusive. Meagan responded to most of the stimuli, but the doctor felt that something just wasn't right. He told us that he thought that Meagan's reactions were due to her keen awareness of her surroundings; he thought that her hearing was impaired. He scheduled advanced testing.

The Children's Hospital and Health Center in San Diego bills itself as "a medical center just for kids." It is the only hospital in San Diego dedicated solely to pediatric care, and it's widely recognized as having one of the leading pediatric audiology programs in the country. We were fortunate to have access to such a renowned facility. After much discussion, we decided that we felt confident with this facility; if anything could be done to help Meagan, surely this would be the place that could do it.

It was an anxiety-filled forty-five minute drive to see the specialists who would definitively answer the questions about Meagan's hearing. In the preceding days, Meagan's mother and I tried very hard to convince each other (and ourselves) that we were mistaken or, at least, that Meagan's hearing loss was minor. We really weren't prepared to hear what we feared we would be told. We were twenty-four years old. Being parents to two children was task enough for us; the prospect of raising a child with special needs was, frankly, terrifying.

The audiology center was quiet. Everyone spoke in a hushed voice. A kind woman—who looked much too young to be an expert at anything—explained the testing procedures to us. I carried Meagan to the other side of the facility, where I handed her to a stranger in scrubs who took her the last few steps into the fish bowl. The technician sat Meagan on the floor and began to play with her. Meagan showed little interest in the toys, but the kind-eyed stranger persisted, and after a few minutes, Meagan was distracted enough to be left alone. The woman disappeared through the heavy, insulated door, closing it behind her, leaving our two-year-old alone in the fish bowl. Her mother and I watched from comfortable padded chairs in a darkened observation room.

The baby aquarium was well-appointed. An elegantly framed picture graced the back wall, and a fake window (complete with an equally fake pastoral scene) graced another. It had all the accoutrements of a child's room—toys, a carpet, even some miniature furniture. It was such a life-like setting that the well-disguised sound baffles covering the three nonglass walls were nearly invisible. The six-foot-tall speakers flanking the couch were the only clue that it wasn't a run-of-the-mill playroom.

Meagan sat on the shag carpet with her back straight and her legs akimbo, looking bewildered and lost. The technician had left toys scattered around her, and many more toys spilled out of the tiny toy box against the wall behind her. Meagan ignored the toys. She chewed on her fist. In her lacy, powder-blue dress and cute little shoes—patent leather Mary Janes—she looked like a baby doll. She chewed on her fist, and she never reacted to the noises that burst from the oversized speakers that sat less than three feet behind her. The sounds were so loud that I heard them in the observation room, after they'd traveled through the baffles and soundproofing materials designed to contain them in the fish bowl. Meagan's mother heard them, too, and I watched her bottom lip tremble as she began to accept what she had feared.

As we watched through the window, it became apparent that our daughter couldn't hear. Our Meagan was a child with special needs. This was daunting news that filled us with sorrow and dread. Doubts and fears raced through my mind. *Had I caused this? Could I fix it? What should I do? What should I do first? What did I need to learn? Was I strong enough to raise a child with special needs? Were my wife and I smart enough? Could we provide our child the things she needed? Would we need help? We almost certainly would, but where would we find it?*

We left the audiology center with an official diagnosis: severe to profound bilateral hearing loss. The little residual hearing Meagan had was useless in human application. Our daughter could stand directly in front of a blaring car horn and not hear it. Even though we had expected it, even though we'd thought we were prepared for it, the diagnosis seemed abrupt, and it was shocking. It left me reeling in uncertainty and apprehension. I resolved that I would be strong, stoic; that was what I thought my family needed.

Meagan's mother became overwhelmed with emotion on the way to the car, and we stopped on the sidewalk outside of the center. The four of us hugged and huddled, and we told each other that everything was okay, that deafness was not insurmountable, that we were resilient. We whispered promises to the baby who couldn't hear them. I pretended to be strong; we made each other feel strong. We had no way of knowing what the future held for us, but we had hope. So we strode into the future with the confidence that only young people can have.

The diagnosis could have been devastating, but we didn't allow it to be. Many families have been destroyed by the challenges of raising a child with special needs, but we weren't. It was challenging, yes, but we grew from the experiences. I think our youth and optimism are what made the difference. Meagan's mother took charge of the situation from the first day. By the time of the follow-up visit with our family doctor three days later, Laural had located a support group, enrolled herself in a sign language course, taught Meagan two signs, scouted preschools for the hearing impaired, and read more books on deafness and hearing than I could count. Laural cut the path, and the rest of us followed.

Part of my personal growth was in learning to see the world through Meagan's eyes. As a result, I began to view others differently; I became more tolerant, especially toward people with disabilities. Although I could never "walk a mile" in someone else's shoes, I could certainly see how the world acted toward and reacted to my daughter. I developed an appreciation for how people who are "different" are treated and for how they make their way through life.

Meagan introduced us to a society we would never have known otherwise. The Deaf culture is unknown to most of the world, but it is rich and intricate with rules and conventions much different from mainstream culture. For instance, turning one's face away from a speaker is the greatest of insults. I learned this the hard way while trying to paint a dresser and carry on a conversation with Meagan and a friend of hers. It was a mistake I never repeated!

My personal growth eventually developed into professional growth. After Meagan grew up and moved out on her own, I began to pursue a new career as a public school teacher. Starting out as a substitute teacher, I found that the easy days at the mainstream schools bored me but that I was thrilled by the challenging, often difficult days at the special education centers. Today, I work only in the centers, and my life is enriched by the students with special needs who teach me—while I teach them—every day.

But the greatest lesson of all came from being Meagan's dad, which taught me that the arrival of a child with special needs is not a reason for sorrow or dread. For me, it was the beginning of a rich and satisfying journey filled with amazing lessons and even more amazing adventures. The experiences I've been blessed with because of Meagan have made me a better parent and a better person.

—D. C. Hall

Jacob's Treasure Map

"Okay, Jacob," said my husband Bart. "Show us you know how to get from the dorm to the main classroom building."

Our college boy slouched in his black T-shirt, almost like a typical eighteen-year-old. "I'll be alright," he insisted. But his father and I and our younger sons Spence and Gabriel winced, each remembering an incident that had taken place two years earlier. An incident Jacob called "ancient history."

Today, our son wore the shiny new label "college freshman," a label we'd thought impossible because of all the other labels that had been stuck on him since early childhood. Our home was in the suburbs three hours away. None of us knew this city. But it was Jacob, who was least able to orient himself, who would have to find his way without us.

Hands in pockets, Jacob stared through his smudged glasses at his Birkenstocks. "Ummmmmm," he started.

That "Ummmmmm," with its familiar cadence, ran through me. It was Jacob's way of buying time, hoping someone else might answer for him. I understood, because I once thought experts could answer my questions about him.

My questions began when Jacob was a baby. I propped an art book in front of him, open to a colorful page. He opened his mouth in baby awe, fixed his eyes on the Matisse, and settled into his seat in rapt attention. My little Buddha, still and silent. I forget how long he stared at that page, but I remember it was far longer than the child-development books called "normal." This thrilled me then. "He's an artist," I told Bart.

But the differences I noticed later felt less promising. When we left him with a babysitter, he didn't cry as expected, and when we returned, he didn't greet us with the squeals and hugs we longed for. My anxiety grew as we noticed that our other-worldly little three-year-old had memorized all the songs on his Raffi tapes, including the ones in French or Spanish, but didn't respond when asked "Jacob, where's the kitty?" When Jacob screamed in frustration over a toy dinosaur that wouldn't stand up properly, I wrapped my arms around him. He pushed me away, repeating something we'd read in a picture book, "Where's my mommy!" "I am your Mommy," I sobbed back.

And so the process began: parking our second son with a babysitter, gathering up the folder marked "Jacob," dragging a tantrumming preschooler away from his perfect lines of dinosaurs for tests, waiting for a report, a label. We wanted a name for it. We thought that if experts could pinpoint the quirks in his brain circuitry, then they could correct them with therapy, medication, and special schools. If there was a name, maybe there'd be a cure. But every time we went back for a follow-up, they came up with a different name.

First, it was "pragmatic language disorder." Then it was "developmental delay." In the years that followed, the labels included pervasive developmental disorder otherwise undifferentiated, nonverbal learning disability, autism, and atypical attention deficit disorder without hyperactivity. Every time, the clinicians said Jacob didn't strictly fit any diagnosis in their books.

Meanwhile, Jacob taught himself to read before he turned five. He spent solitary hours absorbed in thick nonfiction books, studying his "serial obsessions," as Bart and I wryly called them—bats, marine biology, Egyptian mummies, flags. Although he continued to struggle with conversation, he had mastered delivering the informational lecture. In the car, he rattled off facts about Greek mythology, his feet kicking the back of my seat.

"Really?" I responded. "Now, Jacob, please let Spence talk."

When the psychologist said Jacob had made so much progress that we could move him from the preschool for children with autism to a preschool for kids with pre-learning disabilities, we cried and laughed and hugged each other. Later, when they reported he'd outgrown language therapy and when they recommended a mainstream school, we rushed home to tell the grandparents the happy news.

But it still took several disappointments before we found a school that fit, a small independent school that did something I didn't even recognize at the time: treat him as an individual, not a diagnosis. When Jacob's third-grade teacher invited him to explore his current favorite subject and share it with the class, we discovered along with her that, when put in the front of the classroom, his annoying lecturing became something else, an "independent report." Quietly, I allowed myself to have new hopes for him.

One day, while emptying Jacob's jeans pockets before the laundry, I found a piece of paper folded into a thick little packet. I unfolded it four times to find a brightly colored, hand-drawn map. From the X, labeled "Start Here," a circuitous route was marked by arrows. My fingertip traced the path as it meandered up green mountains and over silver bridges, passing along its journey the pyramids, the Kingdom of the Mermaids, a leprechaun, a smiling Cyclops, stick figures labeled "Spence" and "Gabriel," each landmark in a different color, until the path led to a treasure chest. At the top of the page, in his little-boy writing, it read, "Jacob's Treasure Map."

That map took me one step closer to appreciating the unique landscape of Jacob's soul. While I relied on experts to get from here to there, Jacob just knew that there were leprechauns and treasure chests to be discovered somewhere along the scenic route.

By this time, our home had long since become a therapeutic environment, stocked with educational puzzles, games, and equipment borrowed from therapists. I found myself cataloging the hours, asking myself, *Is there more I can teach my son today?*

I did not see the shift coming. It happened when Jacob was about eleven. Over the kitchen table after school, I drilled him on his facial-expression flashcards, teaching him by rote what our other sons had learned by nature.

"Come on, honey, look at the card." I said wearily, holding up a flashcard of a boy, eyes wide, eyebrows lifted, mouth agape.

"Ummmmm," he said.

"Jacob, the card."

"Angry?" asked Jacob.

"No, honey, this is 'surprised.'"

"This is stupid!" He shoved his chair away from the table. "I'll never get it. Face it! I'm a weirdo."

I stood, grabbed him. "I never want to hear you say that word again! You are not a weirdo!"

Eye to eye with him, my hand gripping his thin wrist, I realized that while the experts had been searching for a label for Jacob, he had come up with a label of his own—one that sickened me. I saw the courage it took for him to do all we asked of him every day. I saw that, although I thought I had accepted his disability and although he'd made "remarkable progress," every test took something out of him—no, out of our vision of him. And each time a new report arrived, my husband and I felt like it was a setback. Our other two children were given space and time to develop, but for Jacob, we were handed a hardcopy of his future and somehow we had started to believe it.

Letting go of his wrist, I realized I was tired of it all. I wanted to laugh with him as I laughed with Spence and Gabriel, with no therapeutic agenda. Yet, I couldn't see any other option but to keep walking the road we were on.

It was in another office when Jacob was about twelve that we heard a new label. The psychologist talked with him, looked over the file labeled "Jacob," now as thick as an atlas, and asked, "Has anyone ever mentioned Asperger's syndrome? It's a new diagnosis. I'd like to test him again."

We both knew it at exactly the same time. Professionals could put another label on him, find another diagnosis, but it would not change Jacob or what he could do. His colorful imagination, his courage, his quirky conversation, and social mix-ups—none of that would change just because some doctor gave it a different name. The labels and reports were supposed to guide his therapy, but all they did was make us look at him differently—as someone we were supposed to fix.

Bart and I looked at each other and shook our heads. "No. No more tests. No more labels."

We didn't realize it at the time, but as Bart and I shook our heads, the second part of our journey began.

Unlabeled, Jacob blossomed. He wrote poetry, made pottery, excelled in English and social studies, and worked at a day camp. He joined the drama club, where he learned more from mimicking emotions on the stage than he had ever learned from my facial-expression flashcards.

But in certain ways he still stuck out, and these areas concerned me.

He walked through life with his mind somewhere else, oblivious to his surroundings. He had no sense of direction. On that day I remembered so vividly, when Jacob was sixteen, I'd asked him to walk Gabriel home from Little League practice only four blocks from our house. He made it to the baseball field, but then he and Gabriel got lost walking home. When Jacob called me on his cell phone, admitting they were lost, my chest ached.

Later that year, when Jacob failed the learner's permit test for the third time, he told me, "I just don't think driving is for me." I was relieved and proud that he was being realistic. But I feared this decision would doom him to a future of relying on others to get him from place to place. Where we live in the suburbs, not driving is a serious disadvantage.

But Jacob amazed me, coming up with his own answers. In the spring of junior year, as his classmates visited colleges, I decided my biggest hope was for him to attend a local college. But Jacob had a different idea. His voice husky with excitement, he told me about this college he'd read about, one I'd never heard of. "I think this could be the college for me," he said.

I felt the old fears rising inside me. I understood why the school appealed to him, with its small classes, emphasis on writing instead of testing, and great education department. And I could see in his eyes the allure of a big city with so much to do—plus public transportation, his ticket to independence. It was the only college he applied to, and once he ripped open the fat envelope and shouted, "I got in!" how could I say no?

Now, here we were, waiting for Jacob to lead us to the building where his classes would be.

At the next corner, my new college freshman stopped, looking left and right.

"Is this where we turn?" my husband asked him, his brow wrinkled.

"Ummmmmmm," Jacob said.

I turned away. I told myself that we should have been grateful he had graduated from high school, that we should not have hoped for this.

"Excuse me . . . Need some help?" came a voice from behind me, a man with a moustache and a wide smile.

"We're trying to show our son—" I started, but he was looking at Jacob as if they were old friends.

Jacob answered, his voice deep and clear, with the name of this college he had chosen and the address of the classroom building.

"Oh, I know where that is," said the man. His face was so open, his way so casual, that we followed him.

When we saw the college banner, Jacob's stride lengthened. Just then, I recognized a small shift in myself. I can't say that in that moment I could foresee that Jacob would thrive at college or that he would become—it still gives me chills—a teacher. But maybe I went from accepting Jacob to believing in him. Six years earlier, I had let go of my pursuit of a diagnosis; now I let go of my desire for him to fit into another kind of label, the opposite of weirdo, the very things not on his map. Looking ahead, I saw Jacob had found his college and I knew he would find his way.

—*Faith Paulsen*

Poor Thing

At the movie rental shop, the woman waiting in line looks back at us. Actually, what she does is this: she stares at my daughter Elina. For a fleeting moment, she observes me and my other daughter, Mia, before her eyes fixate once more on Elina. This woman is alone. But if the lady were with a companion, they might start whispering to each other right about now.

Yes, I have seen this scene played out a million times before. With more than seven years of motherhood behind me, I've learned to take this public gawking in stride. I look over at my little wonder, her porcelain-like fingers clutching Fuzzy, her stuffed panda bear. As always, she's curiously looking about, her eyes smiling.

Then comes the inevitable.

The woman turns around, gestures toward Elina, and exclaims, "She's so blonde!"

Why, yes. I could simply nod in agreement. But I know that hidden behind this stranger's obvious observation lurks a question: How in the world did she get all that blonde hair?

When I'm feeling especially playful, I'll answer, "Oh, she's Irish," as if that explained everything. And this is true. Elina was born in Ireland. But people look at us—a brown-haired, olive-skinned Asian-American family with one fair-skinned, blue-eyed child with honey-blonde hair—and they're baffled. Understandably so.

To deepen the mystery, Elina isn't adopted. And she didn't inherit her physical coloring from her daddy. He, too, is Asian with hound-dog eyes, a feature they share in common.

Today, I wink at Elina before responding, "She's Irish."

The woman nods as if considering the explanation, yet her puzzled expression remains.

I let some time pass before adding, "And she also has albinism."

Most people are familiar with "albinos." But one common misunderstanding is that all people with albinism have platinum white hair and red eyes. Elina, among many others, falls into a different category.

I then offer a brief explanation of this genetic condition in which individuals have little or no pigmentation. First, we chat about the obvious concerns of sunburn and skin cancer. Elina, unlike her little sister Mia, never tans. But the primary indicator of albinism—its fundamental challenge—is the presence of certain eye conditions, which vary from individual to individual. Albinism affects the development of the retina and the nerve signals that travel between the eye and the brain. The result is one or a number of visual impairments. In Elina's case, this includes amblyopia (lazy eye), low vision, and nystagmus (involuntary movement of the eyes back and forth). It was her difficulty in tracking objects when she was six weeks old that actually led to the diagnosis of albinism.

At the mention of visual impairment, the woman before me examines Elina more closely and nods. Yes, she now detects something different about the eyes and a slight but noticeable head-shaking from the nystagmus.

From here, I know our interaction will veer in one of two directions. Some people, initially awed and curious, will shift into a serious mode. They will look at Elina and with a voice tinged with deep sadness say, "Oh, poor thing!"

When I'm feeling especially lousy, I might agree with that sentiment. Yes, life with a physical disability can be challenging and frustrating. My daughter has an uphill climb ahead, a great disadvantage.

When we first discovered Elina's condition, we researched as much as we could about albinism. Quite frankly, there's more than enough information out there to overwhelm and devastate any new parent. Common topics revolved around not just the physical challenges but the emotional and social ones as well. We focused on them all. She won't be able to see the intricate details of the world as others can. She won't be able to read without great difficulty. She won't be able to drive. She won't be able to make friends. She won't, she won't, she won't!

But that seems like ages ago, before concrete knowledge and real-life experiences opened our eyes to a different perspective. Since then, we have learned that people with albinism can, indeed, drive with the aid of special visual equipment and enough determination. We have years to find out how this will play out in our lives. But for now, we're content watching Elina surround herself with a circle of kind-hearted friends. To see her cruise up and down the street on her bicycle with confidence. Or to run into a moving jump rope, hopping with even cadence at each turn before effortlessly slipping out, giggling the entire time. She has even developed a love for knitting: scarves, pouches, animals, you name it. And she seems to do everything with complete joy and ease, though nothing about her physical condition has changed. That is, no magical spell has whisked away albinism and its challenges. We still deal with them everyday.

When we look beyond the "special needs," what we witness is a miracle: the blossoming of a child, a human being. Elina is developing in her own way, at her own pace, to be her own person.

Yes, some people will continue to regard Elina as "disabled" or even "abnormal." I understand their point of view. I've been there. But in time, I hope everyone will stretch beyond that limited way of thinking and fully appreciate, as I now can, how each child bears gifts and life lessons to this world.

The woman is now ready to leave the rental shop. Having learned a bit about albinism, she takes one last look at Elina. How will our encounter end? Will she exclaim "Poor thing!" or throw us a look of pity?

Elina fingers the display atop the counter before moving on to the colorful assortment of goodies on nearby shelves. Her little sister Mia follows. With Fuzzy still under her care, Elina pauses to smile at me, her eyes beaming.

"Well." The woman shakes her head. Before stepping out the door, she gestures toward both girls and says with a flourish, "They're both just beautiful!"

Well, yes. That is absolutely true.

—Ritz Imuta

We're In This Together

At the close of every yoga class, soothing music plays softly in the background, inducing the mind to think peaceful thoughts. But for me, that never happens. Usually, the room turns cold and I become restless. At the last class, I tried to warm my body by rubbing my hands against my legs and felt the outline of an old leg scar. I settled into a trance, allowing the music to conjure up memories about the scar and my mentally challenged brother. What a weird place to go during relaxation pose—a time I typically spend reviewing my to-do list.

Closing my eyes, I envisioned my childhood home in Memphis, Tennessee. Soon, an image rose clearly to my consciousness. I was twelve years old standing inside my bedroom. I stood in front of a white vanity table draped in a wraparound skirt of lavender and white checks that my mother had sewn, intending to dress it up, hide stored items underneath, and match the newly painted lavender walls. Yellow sunlight streamed through the window, spotlighting a group of young girls: me, my sister, and our two best friends. Suddenly, my youngest brother bolted through the doorway. Boys were not allowed inside our room; "Keep Out" read the sign posted on the door. And Greg was a particularly hyperactive boy who blew through a room, twisting and turning at tornado speeds, destroying everything in his pathway. So we set about rounding him up, like sheep dogs, herding him out of our bedroom.

Funny, how a flashback never has sound—just the physical images of long-ago characters playing out like a silent home movie. I saw myself chase my brother past the vanity, at which point a loose nail, protruding from the lavender skirt, caught my left thigh, cutting a deep, bloody gash. I let out a silent screech. Then the movie ended.

Today, that vanity is long gone, the lavender room is gone, and in a sense, those teenage girls are gone, but the scar on my left leg is still there. After my flashback, I was awakened to other hidden scars linked to my brain-damaged brother.

Gregory Lee Walker was born August 14, 1959. At three months old, Greg received the DTP vaccine (diphtheria, tetanus, and pertussis). Within weeks, the normal life handed to him at birth was abruptly shattered. The viruses my brother was supposed to be vaccinated against were the exact infections the shot introduced into his body—whooping cough and encephalitis—attacking his normal brain like an intense storm, leaving behind unspecified damages.

Greg was given the first shot in October and the second shot the last week of November. The first symptoms appeared in mid-December, when he started coughing, crying, and losing sleep. On January 7th, he was admitted to LeBonheur Children's Hospital under quarantine, a culture was taken that showed my brother was in the fourth week of whooping cough. He remained in the hospital for ten days; my mother was at his side the entire time.

I was five years old, my sister was six, and our oldest brother was eight. While entrusted to the care of our doting grandmother, our every need was met and our health and well-being were intact, yet we were still young enough to believe that the world began and ended with our parents. We felt homesick for our mother.

Finally, Greg was released. No one was more excited than my older brother, sister, and me. We had our mother back. Life would be normal again.

By March, once again something wasn't right. My brother couldn't sleep, and at seven and half months old, he couldn't turn over or sit up. He cried for hours. His tiny fists knotted up, punching the air, and he clawed at his forehead. My mother noticed his forehead was swollen and the soft spot on top of his head wasn't closing up properly. On March 30th, Greg was hospitalized again at Lebonheur Children's Hospital, where a pediatric neurologist tested fluid from my brother's spine. The test came back positive for encephalitis. The fluid was then drained from Greg's spine and brain through his soft spot.

"I'll never forget that day," my mother recently told me. "When they brought him back to the hospital room, he woke up, rolled over, and stood up in the crib and laughed for the first time in his life."

Greg's physical pain was gone. But the doctor said he couldn't say how much damage had been done, only that it was in the frontal lobe of his brain. "Greg may never walk or talk," the doctor said.

My mother wouldn't settle for broken. She talked to any and every doctor who would listen. She studied and researched until she understood the malfunctions of Greg's brain. Her rescue efforts were like those in the movie *Forrest Gump.* During a battle scene in Vietnam, with bombs exploding all around Gump's platoon, instead of running away,

Gump runs back into the middle of the explosions to carry out his buddies. That's what my mother continued to do with my brother. In the middle of each battle, she carried Greg out of the jungle. But there were others in the jungle, too—my oldest brother, my sister, and me. Sometimes we needed rescuing, too, but it felt like no one ever came. Like the time when Greg was in the hospital, our hearts ached for our mother.

My dad explained my brother's condition by comparing the brain to the old telephone switchboards from the early 1900s. "Operators used to sit in front of huge panels called peg boards," he said. "They connected phone calls by plugging a wire into a tiny hole in the boards. In your brother's brain, there are wires that will never be connected."

One of the disconnections involved behavior. My brother could not sit calmly at the dinner table, watch TV, or even scribble in a coloring book. Greg was like the Energizer Bunny, running constantly at full speed.

The first thing Mother had to do was find a way to calm him. She found a doctor who prescribed him a drug almost unheard of at the time—Ritalin. For us, Ritalin was a miracle drug. But like the calm before the storm, everything was peaceful until the medicine wore off.

There were no instructions on how to deal with my little brother. Dr. Spock wrote a book full of advice about parenting children. But no chapters in Spock's book were about parenting a child like Greg. Nor was there a chapter explaining the effects that Greg's demanding needs had on our family.

Many times I wondered, "Why did this happen to my brother? And why did this happen to our family?"

My mother would sometimes read us a poem, "Heaven's Very Special Child." It's about a meeting held in heaven in which the angels ask the Lord for a special family with whom to place a special child. "So God chose us, because we're special," my mother would explain.

I used to think, *If special means something is wrong, then something must be wrong with our whole family, and that's why we were chosen. So what are people thinking about us?*

My mother openly accepted the role as the chosen parent of a child with special needs. Every day was a new battle, and every day there was a need to rescue Greg from the jungle. At times, my mother looked wounded, and I worried about who would rescue her. She would calm my fears by saying, "God is with me, giving me strength. So don't worry; everything will be okay." But sometimes, late at night, my sister and older brother would hear our mother crying, pouring her heart out to our dad. Maybe God was with my mother, but when trapped in the jungle, it was Daddy who rushed in and carried my mother out.

Once, when Greg was three years old and I was eight, he was allowed a rare opportunity to play outside with me and a group of children. For some reason, Greg threw a small metal car, striking another child in the head. The child screamed as if he had been hit by a boulder. Out of fear, I panicked. I struck my brother on the back—again and again and again. I couldn't stop; I just kept hitting him as if I could knock the mental retardation out of his body. My mother raced across the yard in tears, scooped up my brother, and took him inside. I was left alone in the jungle, shaken. My heart was as bruised as the child whose head had been struck by the toy car. Perhaps my brain was broken like my brother's. Maybe more. After all, who beats a defenseless, developmentally disabled, three-year-old little boy? I wanted my mother to retrieve me like my brother and fix my broken brain.

Occasionally, kids would pass through the field behind our house. If my brother was outside, they would yell through the chain-link fence: "Hey, retard!"

Those words would bring me to my knees. I felt as though my brother's heart had been transplanted inside my chest; I could feel the pain of his defects.

Another time, a small neighbor boy stood on the curb and hollered across the street at my brother, "You can't come in my yard. You're retarded."

Such comments were among the bombs dropping in our jungle. I desperately wanted to be rescued. *Where was God?* I wondered. *Does he not know our family is wounded and in need of his help?*

When Greg started school, my mother researched the special education teachers at the public schools and decided which teachers best fit his needs. For years, my parents and Greg slaved over homework. Consequently, he did better than what anyone had expected. It was a rocky road, but at age twenty-one, he walked down the aisle, smiling with excitement in his cap and gown, to accept a "special" high school diploma. Later, he went on to work at the Sheltered Occupational Workshop for the mentally retarded, where today, at age forty-nine, he still works.

For years, I prayed my family would be restored back to its original design with both parents doting over four healthy children. After all, the Scripture says that you can have life and you can have it abundantly. In my mind, those words held only one meaning—a promise that God would heal, repair, and restore my life. But nothing ever changed.

Then I read about the reappearance of Jesus among his followers after his death. So filled with grief and disappointment, they failed to recognize him. It wasn't until Jesus revealed the wounds on his side and on his hands that they knew his true identity. Their preconceived ideas about what a victorious God should look like changed once Christ became known through his scars . . . scars he bore for loving his family—us.

The nail scar on my leg is minuscule compared to the invisible scars inside me, my brothers, my sister, and my parents. The constant battles in the jungle left us with scars as permanent as birthmarks. Filled with my own grief and disappointment, I had failed to see that Jesus kept his scars. Only later in my life did I recognize that they were his way of saying, "We're in this together."

Like those early believers, I've stopped grieving the loss of the idyllic life I had created in my dreams. Seeing my own wounds, I recognized myself. Like Christ, I, too, have become known for the scars I bear from loving my family. And for that I am blessed.

—Debbi Wise

Square Pegs

A square peg. That is how we describe someone who is different, someone eccentric, free-thinking, unconventional, unusual, or downright odd. Most likely, you know one or more square pegs. Maybe you are related to one. Maybe you are raising one or more. Maybe you are one yourself. In my case, it's all three. I am the product of a family of square pegs; my mother is a shamanic healer, my grandfather an eclectic artist, and my grandmother a passionate actress. The gene pool that my cellular self went fishing in at conception yielded some interesting traits, which, as I grew up, made me feel both blessed and cursed.

I was a creative little kid, reveling in theatrics and dance, and I loved to write stories and poems. I was even more enthusiastic when it came to arts and crafts; to this day, the heady scent of a fresh box of crayons drives me half-mad with joy. What seemed to go hand-in-hand with my highly active imagination, however, was a moody, emotional, very distractible, and often anxious mind. As a teenager, this heightened sensitivity triggered depressive episodes and avoidant behavior, causing my confidence to plummet. I felt upset by the different drummer I heard, terribly out-of-step with the world; I wanted to march in time with everyone else.

Well into adulthood, I searched for answers to many tough questions: Why do I feel so different? Why does no one else seem as overwhelmed as I? Do I need to change myself so I can fit in?

When I became a mother, the answers began to appear but not in ways I could have had anticipated. When our first son, Tanner, was born, I considered myself to be your typical, miracle-blessed, chronically tired new mother. I delighted in him, swooned with love for him, and proudly wrote down his achievements and milestones throughout the first year.

As he grew into a toddler, however, I began to notice that my son was developing differently from the other children his age. At times, he did not seem aware of people around him, preferring to play alone, and he was extremely sensitive to sounds and coarse textures. At the same time, he was keenly intelligent; at age two and a half, he was writing his full name with fat, colored crayons and reciting the name of each color over and over again. When he began to talk in full sentences, his speech sounded stilted and formal, and often the things he said were lines taken directly from television commercials and children's shows. As the list of unusual traits lengthened, we began to realize that our son was truly different. Our concern led us to a consultation with a pediatric neurologist when Tanner was five, and as a result of many tests and observations, he was diagnosed with Asperger's syndrome, a form of autism. His behavior finally made sense. We had our very own little square peg.

What struck me then was the realization that I did not want to "fix" my son. I liked him as he was—a gentle, unusual, surprising soul. To try to drastically change him would change the child I knew and loved. Instead of attempting to whittle our square peg into a round one through experimental medications or intensive therapies, we decided to focus on helping him know, understand, and accept himself. We realized we would need to teach him how to succeed as an autist in a predominantly non-autist society.

I cannot claim that it has been easy. Schools, friends, and even family members can have strong opinions as to what is best for a child who is wired differently. We have had to push for accommodations when needed in his school, and we've had the heartache of watching him struggle to understand a world that has an innate unspoken language intrinsically different from his own.

Our goals thus far have been realized, as Tanner is currently in a typical eighth grade classroom, living successfully as his very authentic self.

Son number two arrived in our world around the same time as Tanner's diagnosis. John was a chubby, good-natured baby who, when unhappy, wielded a scream that could strip paint from the walls. For Tanner, learning to share space (and Mom) with his younger brother was a stimulating learning experience. His sensory issues were repeatedly challenged by his screeching baby brother, who quickly grew into a noisy, grabbing toddler and later a chatty, active little boy. Watching John develop allowed us to experience what most parents do: our child reaching typical milestones at the appropriate times, with no signs of unusual behaviors. It was a relief to realize John would not have to suffer the same trials we knew Tanner would face as he grew.

Life with these two little men was busy and full, and certainly unusual. We quickly learned what a family of a child with special needs can reasonably handle, and which activities and events might be better left for those with more energy and patience. We suffered through many failed efforts trying to keep up with the typical families around us. Going to the movies or to dinner was not even a possibility. Signing Tanner up for basketball camp resulted in seventy dollars down the drain, after he spent the better part of two weeks hunkered down under the bleachers, his fingers stuck in his ears. A trip to a local farm was cut short after Tanner heard a cow mooing and reacted with flood of tears and panic-stricken howling. Even the wind blowing in his hair could be enough to overwhelm him, which precluded beach visits and many other outdoor experiences. Still, we managed to make our own fun, and we celebrated each coping skill Tanner developed, helping him open new windows to the world around him as he grew.

Though sometimes dark, Nature has a sense of humor: Shortly after we decided two children was a barely manageable number and that perhaps we should stop there, we found out son number three was already on the way.

Adam was born after a high-risk pregnancy and an emergency cesarean section. The drama of his birth was counterbalanced by the first eighteen months with him, when he was a happy, active baby. In the wake of Tanner's experience, I had been hyper-vigilant about childhood milestones, so when Adam was still not speaking at nineteen months, I consulted a developmental specialist. Adam began to receive speech therapy at home, very quickly acquiring new words. Soon, he could not seem to stop talking.

As he grew older, he could not seem to stop moving, either. By the time he was four, Adam was a tumultuous, noisy blur of manic movement and boisterous sound, with a personality that had the intensity of a blast furnace. He was charming, extremely creative, and perpetually curious, but simply being near him was exhausting. He radiated a frenetic energy that seemed to propel him through his days. We tried hard to be patient with his non-stop demands for interaction and conversation, but often we were overwhelmed and fell into bed utterly drained by day's end.

Adam's over-the-top behavior continued once he began school, and in the classroom, it was even more of a problem. Adam was excitable, distracted, and prone to outbursts, tantrums, and aggressive behavior. He was unable to build friendships and quickly became depressed and talked of self-harm. In an effort to understand what was happening to our bright little boy, we took him to be evaluated by a child psychiatrist. At age five, after many tests and observations both in school and at home, Adam was diagnosed with pediatric bipolar disorder and attention deficit hyperactivity disorder (ADHD). I was in disbelief.

We now had another square peg to add to our collection.

What challenges could we expect with this child? The information we found on the Internet about his diagnosis provided little comfort. Statistics on teen suicide and the side effects of medicines filled message boards, where parents shared stories of their beloved children being arrested or placed in locked facilities. Encouraging words of advice were scarce among the parental logs; most seemed to be looking for help getting through their own moments of crisis. This was making Asperger's syndrome look like a walk in the park!

I mentally took stock of the things we would need to raise this extraordinary child. Hope? Yes, we would certainly need that. Faith? That, too, seemed essential. A sense of humor? Without that, we would not stand a chance!

As my Internet searching continued, I unearthed something I had not expected. I slowly realized the symptoms of bipolar disorder were eerily familiar.

They seemed to describe not only the landscape of my son's mind but my own as well. Racing thoughts, cycles of depression and bursts of intense inspiration, difficulty concentrating . . . as I read on, I knew a visit to a professional was in order. Often, it is only when tracing back through family medical history in an effort to understand the child does a parental diagnosis come to light. In trying to understand and help my youngest son, I was at last able to better understand myself.

After being diagnosed with bipolar disorder II, I was placed on a mood stabilizer, just like Adam. The difference it made in all our lives cannot be downplayed. For the first time, I was able to embrace my "otherness," relieved it had a name, and I was eager to learn more about how it affected me. The medication lifted my depression and enabled me to focus on advocating for Adam, whose behavior had significantly improved. But we still felt that he, like Tanner, needed to have all the advantages of learning those skills that would allow him to remain his most authentic self once he was grown.

After learning all we could about special education law, we fought a difficult battle to have Adam placed in a therapeutic school. After years of struggle, fighting the system, we were victorious. Today, Adam is working above grade level in a specialized setting, and each day he gains effective skills that allow him to keep his more dramatic behaviors in check.

The square peg? I have learned to see the beauty in its shape and texture and to know the value of its determined resistance to the round hole by which we often measure ourselves. I was given the unexpected responsibility of parenting two sons with special needs, stumbling into the role without warning or training, yet expected and needing to rally and not only do the job but do it well. I discovered that disappointing setbacks and moments of unbearable frustration were to be expected. I learned where to find the support our family needed as well as some powerful tactics for weathering each storm we encountered.

The most unexpected lesson learned, though, was the realization that we have been blessed by this experience. Every day with my sons, I encounter powerful moments of trust, hope, perseverance, and unconditional love. I watch as they demonstrate loyalty to one another, practice tolerance, and take each day as it comes. Life with my square-peg family brings the opportunity to celebrate the joys of being different, to press on in the face of adversity, and to honor our unique, authentic selves.

—Nicole Derosier

A Real Home

"Welcome your new brother home," my parents urged as they placed Louis in the crib that stood at the foot of their bed.

I reached out my small hand and touched the sole of his soft foot, ran my fingers along his five round toes. "Welcome home."

Born prematurely and in need of surgery to repair an improperly formed esophagus, Louis also had been diagnosed with Down syndrome. Back then, in 1964, less was understood about the capabilities of those born with developmental disability, and many babies with this condition were institutionalized rather than brought home. However, my parents did not consider that option. Louis would be raised at home.

Thanks to my parents love and tenacity, Louis, now in his forties, had grown into a happy, healthy, bright adult. He had graduated from a special education school and then did a short stint in a workshop until he received an invitation to participate in a newly created adult day program administered by another organization. While his ability to learn during his school years had consistently amazed our parents, his continued growth in the day program was nothing short of monumental. Under the staff's nurturing care, his reading and writing skills, logic, and memory had grown keen. Once frail and unhealthy, Louis now boasted an athletic frame. He enjoyed swimming and bowling and never missed a shot in basketball. He had a lively sense of humor and was dubbed "class clown." Socially, he had blossomed and was well liked by staff and peers.

Yet, there was a laundry list of things that Louis could not perform independently. He would never be able to drive. He lacked the ability to handle money properly on a consistent basis. He could not self-administer medication when needed. His cooking privileges had been revoked after the third burned pot. In short, Louis could never live without supervision.

With the exception of the year prior to her death, my mother had always been primary caregiver for Louis in the family home. Dad stepped in during her illness, but now nearing eighty years old, he found the responsibilities overwhelming. I volunteered to help, and guardianship was assigned to me. Yet, with my own home and family and a nine-to-five job, the most I could do for Louis was to shuttle him to doctor appointments, prepare the special meals he required, and do some light housekeeping. It wore on me, but I could see it wore more on Louis. He missed the extracurricular activities and weekend visits with friends he had once enjoyed. Now, after his day at the program for adults with special needs, Louis generally sat in his room and listened to the radio, venturing out only at mealtimes. His mischievous hazel eyes dulled, and he became pale. When I noticed he had lost a sizeable amount of weight, I decided it was time to seek out the advice of our family doctor.

"He needs to live in a community residence," the doctor advised matter-of-factly. "He needs the friendship, the stimulation of his peers. He's wasting away sitting in his room alone."

Community residences for the disabled had opened in our county in the mid-1970s, but available placements were few and far between. Louis had been on a waiting list for several years without so much as a nibble. Preference was rightly given to those in the most desperate of circumstances, and now, as my father and I watched Louis become increasingly more withdrawn, we felt desperate, too. His doctor was right: Louis needed a place where he was not simply "maintained" but could continue to grow. I knew a home with his peers was the right situation, but I had concerns. I wanted the very best for Louis: a place he could share with a caring family, a place where those in charge always had his best interests at heart, a place where he would always feel welcome as he walked through the front door. A real home.

Despite my concerns, I continued to advocate for Louis' placement. Finally, his name reached the top of the residential waiting list at his program. Still, month after month passed without our receiving a call telling us that a room was available. I attended all the meetings and workshops on community residence placement that were offered, exhausted my contacts in the field, and then one day was simply told by an official that there were just no foreseeable openings becoming available any time soon. That night I lay my head on my pillow and worried myself to sleep with visions of my fading brother swirling through my head. The next day, I started to pray.

Within a few weeks, a call came. There was an opening in a ten-bed residence at the far end of the county. Would I be interested, the social worker asked? I answered "yes," though with a great deal of trepidation. The residence seemed so large, so far away. The situation just didn't feel right for Louis.

Were my concerns logical, I asked myself, *or was I having a difficult time letting go of my brother?* A short while later, I received word that the placement had been given to one of Louis' best friends, someone equally as deserving. I felt a touch of disappointment overshadowed by relief.

That summer, some changes came for Louis. Based on his performance in the day program, he had been selected to participate in a newly opened "hub site" housed in a local storefront that had been renovated into a chic art gallery. There, participants were given the opportunity to focus on their creative abilities through art projects that would be placed on sale to the general public. In addition, participants were more widely integrated into the community—for example, by attending functions at a nearby library and buying art supplies and through various volunteer activities in the area. Soon Louis became more outgoing, and his old wit returned. The added stimulation of this more active routine began to bring him out of his doldrums.

In the early fall, Dad and I received an invitation to the art gallery's grand opening event. Though Dad no longer left the house often, he surprised me by insisting that he wanted to attend. So we did, along with the families of other program participants, some local business owners, a handful of town politicians, and the managers of the organization that administered the program. When we arrived, a smiling Louis bounded toward us to lead us on the grand tour. He took my hand and proudly pointed out his paintings as other visitors mulled about, admiring the artists' show of talent and skill. At the tour's completion, Louis rejoined his friends and my father ambled toward the buffet lunch line while I stopped to chat with some of the participants' family members that I knew. Suddenly, I noticed Dad wave an excited hand toward me, and I excused myself from the conversation to join him. I was as surprised as Dad to find that the man who stood next to him was not another parent, as he had assumed, but none other than the organization's executive director!

"Your dad has been explaining to me that you're seeking residential placement for Louis," the white-haired gentleman began. "We have an opening in a six-bed residence about five miles away. Call my office tomorrow, and we'll start the process."

Exhilarated, we gave Louis the news that evening. He wasn't happy. Community residence living, it seemed to him, was a good idea for the future but wasn't such a great prospect in the present. Having never been away from home for any extended amount of time, Louis was wary of living in a different house. In the hope of assuaging Louis' fears, we arranged for a dinner visit to the residence. None of us were prepared for what we found behind the stately white colonial's front door.

First, we were greeted by a hearty staff of smiling, outgoing caregivers. We then met the five other residents, three of whom I recognized as Louis' friends from the hub site. Next, we were shown Louis' bedroom, beautifully furnished and immaculately kept. Then my brother went to join his friends at the dinner table as Dad and I were ushered to the living room, where we sat in conversation with the house manager, a lively young woman in her late twenties.

"What are they eating for dinner?" Dad asked, his eyebrows knitted in concern. "Louis has digestive problems and eats a special, chopped diet."

The young woman smoothed her dark hair, "Today, they're having chopped turkey, broccoli, and sweet potatoes. Is that okay for Louis?"

Dad and I looked at each other and smiled. "That's his favorite meal," I chimed.

Bending closer, the house manager said in a low voice, "Three of our other residents have the same health concern as Louis, so as a rule, we provide special meals for them. We're used to that here."

After dinner, Louis came bounding toward us. "Come see the dinner table," he insisted.

Dad and I shot each other a questioning look and followed him. His friends, the house manager explained, had insisted on making Louis a personalized placemat to welcome him. There at the head of the table sat a laminated placement carefully decorated with autumn leaves colored red, gold, and green and across the top emblazoned in bold letters read "Louis."

On the drive home, we asked Louis how he liked the house.

"Oh, it's nice," he said. "I like my room."

"What about dinner?" Dad asked.

"Mmm, the food was good," Louis answered as he rubbed his stomach.

The next day, Dad and I discussed how perfect the residence seemed to be for Louis in each and every detail. There had been so many coincidences that had accompanied Louis' placement that I was inclined to credit divine intervention: Dad had just happened to stand next to the executive director at the art gallery opening; there just happened to be an available space in a local residence; Louis' favorite foods had unwittingly been served during dinner. Even the name of the street where the house was located, Maria Drive, was the same name as Dad's mother, Grandma Maria. Was it too perfect, we wondered as our old fears crept into our thoughts once again? Could the staff there provide a real home for all six residents, or would the arrangement lose its luster after time?

All I can say is that, two years later, Louis continues to thrive and grow as a human being. The staff members have consistently treated Louis with the utmost respect and care and have skillfully nursed him through illness. He participates in sports activities with his peers, regularly attends dances, and has gone on several day trips, after which he phones Dad or me to fill us in on the enjoyments of his day. We still see Louis on a regular basis. He visits Dad often on weekends and on holidays. But when I drive him back to the community residence on the quiet street that shares our grandmother's name, I know Louis has a good home. A real home.

—*Monica A. Andermann*

A fictitious street name has been used in this story to protect the privacy of the people who live and work at the residential facility mentioned therein.

It Is Enough

I could tell before the geneticist said the words out loud that the results were positive. As she recapped each of her suspicions that had led to the blood test two weeks before, she nodded, almost imperceptibly. Little tiny yeses all building up to the big one.

"So," she finally said, "it's confirmed. Truman has Williams syndrome."

Truman was only seven months old at the time, but we'd already learned that he had a penchant for hitting long odds. At three weeks old, he'd been diagnosed with neuroblastoma, a rare pediatric cancer. A tumor grew rapidly in his neck, compressing his airway. He spent his first Christmas on a ventilator in a medically induced coma, and underwent surgery on December 26. He was still recovering when his cardiologist, who'd been monitoring what she believed was an innocent murmur he was sure to outgrow, suddenly became not so sure and ordered an angiogram of the blood vessels in his heart.

Narrowed blood vessels are a hallmark of Williams syndrome. But cancer isn't. A renowned expert on the disorder assured us that being stricken with both was just bad luck.

"It's the statistical equivalent of being struck by lightning," she said. "Twice."

As we waited for the results of the genetic testing, I couldn't help but search the Internet for information.

I found a site listing its symptoms. Pulmonary stenosis? Check. Small chin? Check. Slow weight gain? Check. A star-like splash of white in the iris? Oh, God! Check. The list of common characteristics was coming together like pieces in a puzzle, and the image staring back was my son.

Still, we swayed back and forth. *No, it can't be. It might be. No, things like that don't happen to people like us.* I had no concept of the type of people these things did happen to. I just knew it wasn't us.

After the geneticist broke the news, she assured us that it wasn't caused by anything we had done before his conception or during my pregnancy. It was a transcription error, like a computer file that gets corrupted when you try to copy it. Then she walked us through each organ system and how this accident in his DNA—a minuscule deletion of just twenty of a human's 30,000 genes—might affect him.

Williams syndrome is an odd mix of highs and lows. People with WS are often gifted in language, with colorful and exquisite vocabularies so distinctive they are a favorite study of the world's linguists. Yet, their eloquence belies a cognitive profile that falls in the mildly to moderately retarded range; at best, their intelligence is low average.

As we discussed our son's prognosis with the doctor, I wondered if some parents cry when they receive this kind of news. I studied the doctor's face. I had a feeling that she didn't have any children of her own. Could she have any sense of what we were feeling?

I didn't want to cry in front of her. I wanted to be cool, unflappable. *I'll show her I can handle this,* I thought.

"This changes nothing, and it changes everything," I said stoically. "He is still our baby, and we're going to take him home now and treat him just as we did before."

I didn't cry until we were safely in the car. The first two weeks were a blur. We did all of the things the geneticist suggested: stepped up our early intervention therapies, joined the national advocacy association, reached out to other parents of children with Williams syndrome. But at night, when I should have been sleeping, I spent hours thinking about the future. My husband confessed that he had been waking up at dawn, and while the rest of us slept, he would stare at Truman and weep.

The books on having a child with special needs that I took home from the library said that it's normal to "mourn" the loss of the ideal child you thought you would have. Grieve for him or her, they suggested. But that didn't feel right. My son was alive and here, and while his heart defect was moderate compared to some of the severe cases we'd heard about, it was still potentially life-threatening. And he'd already survived cancer. Cancer! After coming so close to losing him, did I have the audacity to mourn him just because he'll never drive a car?

But what would his, and our, life be like? We worried about the future, about kids making fun of him, about whether he could graduate high school, about the reality that he would probably never be able to live independently. New evidence, made possible by breakthroughs in genetic analysis, suggested that some people with WS might have fewer genes deleted, which, logically, implied that they would have a less severe case. We pursued more testing and visited more experts, in the hope they might tell us what the future would hold for our son.

"I've never met a Williams adult who could count change," one doctor told us. A few minutes later, she held out new hope: "But I can't wait to see the kids who are being diagnosed today, as babies, when they grow up. With earlier diagnoses and interventions, they might have completely different outcomes."

At the same time, I was just trying to enjoy my baby. Our firstborn had gone from her first tooth to first loose tooth in what felt like minutes. We'd already agreed Truman would be our last child, and I knew that, with time, this diagnosis, this punch to the gut that felt fresh each day, would eventually just become part of me. I didn't want to look back with regret later. I went back to savoring those precious morning nursing sessions when just he and I were awake, to laughing as he tasted his own toes, to huffing the sweet scent on the back of his neck.

It's not that it didn't hurt anymore. It did, and the pain still resurfaces sometimes out of nowhere. Normal scenes from everyday life can plunge me into sadness. I watched my niece blow out the candles on her high school graduation cake, with a bright future at a prestigious college ahead of her, and felt my heart tear as I realized Truman would never be standing there.

By the time Truman turned one, the worst of the medical crises were over. After one year, the likelihood of the cancer recurring was practically zero.

His heart was stable. All that was left for him to do was to grow and to learn, all on his own time.

At Truman's first birthday party, with twenty or so members of our family and close friends belting out a heartfelt chorus of "Happy Birthday," I choked back tears. These were the people who'd given us rides to the hospital, made us meals when we were too exhausted, and sent up countless prayers on our behalf. Truman may not have a genius IQ, but he has people who will move the Earth for him. He will not teach astrophysics, but he will teach us incredible, unexpected lessons about our own courage and our capacity to love.

After the party, when the last guests finally left, I put Truman to bed and watched him sleep for a long time—full belly, warm bed, completely content. I didn't feel that heavy weight in my chest anymore. I felt something new, this time in my gut. *This is going to be okay*, it said.

The next morning, I shared this enlightenment with my best friend in an e-mail: "I'm not just putting on a brave face anymore," I wrote. "I totally accept and love my child for who he is. I have no regrets that he is not the person we 'thought' we had created. He is exactly who he is supposed to be, and it is good enough."

—*Kris Cambra*

Contributors

Christa B. Allan ("One in Eight Hundred") lives in Abita Springs, Louisiana, and teaches high school. She is the mother of five and the grammy of three. Her essays have been published in two anthologies, and her first novel is slated for publication in 2010.

Monica A. Andermann ("A Real Home") is a writer who lives on Long Island with her husband/proofreader Bill and their cat Charley. Her work has appeared in various literary journals and newspapers and in *A Cup of Comfort® for Cat Lovers.*

Elizabeth Aquino ("Invisible Child") is a writer living in Los Angeles, California, with her husband and three young children. She is a founder of the nonprofit organization Parents Against Childhood Epilepsy *(www.paceusa.org)* and works actively in health-care advocacy for children with special needs. Her writing has been published in newspapers, magazines, and literary journals.

Louise Beech ("Delilah's Not Diabetic") lives with her husband, two children, one rabbit, one guinea pig, and three fish in Yorkshire, England. She gave up her job in travel when her daughter Katy was diagnosed with juvenile diabetes, but still writes a long-running weekly column for the United Kingdom newspaper, the *Hull Daily Mail*, and has had fiction published in numerous magazines.

Pam Bostwick ("He Believed I Could Fly") has been widely published in magazines, newspapers, and anthologies. Although she is legally blind and hearing impaired, her life is abundant. She enjoys her country home in Banks, Oregon, the beach, playing guitar, doing church work, and being a volunteer counselor. She has seven children and ten grandchildren, and happily remarried on 7/7/07.

Caren Hathaway Caldwell ("Disorderly Conduct") has been a pastor, teacher, reporter, social worker, and community organizer. She lives in Ashland, Oregon, with her partner, Rich Rohde, a community organizer, and their two adopted sons, now seventeen and twenty-one. She advocates throughout Southern Oregon for children with mental illness and their families. For further information about police responses to people with mental illnesses, go to Crisis Intervention Team Resource Center at *www.nami.org.*

Kris Cambra ("It Is Enough") is a science and medicine writer at the Warren Alpert Medical School of Brown University. Her work has been recognized by the Association of American Medical Colleges and the Council for Advancement and Support of Education. She resides in southeastern Massachusetts with her husband and two children. To learn more about Williams syndrome: *www.williams-syndrome.org.*

Ann Campanella ("The Things I Could Not Change"), a resident of Huntersville, North Carolina, is a stay-at-home mom who writes in her spare time. She has published two books of poetry and is working on a third as well as a memoir. She feels a deep connection to her brother with special needs, Richard, and wouldn't change a thing about him.

Harriet Heydemann Cellini ("A Place in the Class") works as a marketing research consultant. She lives near San Francisco,

California, with her husband Gary and daughter Gabriela. This is her first time in print.

Linda S. Clare ("Me and My Beautiful Mother") is the author of several nonfiction books, including her debut novel, *The Fence My Father Built* (Abingdon Press, August 2009). She lives in Eugene, Oregon, with her husband and five wayward cats.

Nicole Derosier ("Square Pegs") is an artist and author living in Stratford, Connecticut, with her husband and three sons. A graduate of the Corcoran College of Art and Design, Nicole spent several years as a teacher before switching to full-time parenting. She steals time in her art studio whenever her busy life allows. For more information on pediatric bipolar disorder: BpKids.org.

Gerry Di Gesu ("Thank You for This Boy, Amen") is a retired school secretary who lives in Union, New Jersey. Her essays and poems have appeared in a wide variety of publications, and her book, *Keep Quiet, You're Only a Girl*, was published in 2004.

Leesa Gehman ("Something in Common") is an administrative assistant and perpetual graduate student in Northeastern Pennsylvania, who hopes to one day work with children with special needs.

Elizabeth King Gerlach ("Reach and Pull") lives in Oregon. She is the author of two award-winning books, *Autism Treatment Guide* and *Just This Side of Normal: Glimpses into Life with Autism*. Nick, her son with special needs, is now twenty-two, working, and living semi-independently.

Ronelle Grier ("Funny-Looking Kid") is a creative nonfiction writer and a contributor to local and national publications. She is a two-time recipient of the National Jewish Press Association's Simon Rockower Award for her feature articles published in the *Detroit Jewish News*. Her background also includes marketing, public relations, and technical writing. She lives with her three children in West Bloomfield, Michigan.

Jennifer Gunter ("Thump, Thump, Kerthump") is a physician, mother, wife, and writer. She lives with her family in Northern California. She is having the time of her life hunting for giant squid in tide pools and developing the first ever flying ice-cream truck. Her first book, *The Preemie Primer: A Doctor and Mother's Guide to Prematurity*, will be published in 2009.

D. C. Hall ("Hearing Hope") lives in Broward County, Florida. The father of three is semi-retired. He's pursuing a career teaching in public schools and specializes in learning centers for children with special needs.

Cynthia Agricola Hinkle ("Finding Rest, Off-Center") is an inspirational writer and author of the children's Arch® books, *The Thankful Leper* and *Star of Wonder*. Her work also appears in several anthologies, including *A Cup of Comfort® Devotional for Mothers*. Living in Georgia, she loves shopping for three adult children and their father. To relax, the family listens to music. A soothing music resource for special families is *www.musicforthesoul.org*.

Erika Hoffman ("Le Mot Juste"), of Chapel Hill, North Carolina, received her B.A. in English and French literature from Duke University, where she also earned her M.A.T. in English education. She has taught in New Jersey, Georgia, and North Carolina. An award-winning writer, she has published nonfiction stories in several anthologies and articles in numerous magazines. A photo of hers recently appeared in *The Rambler*.

Ritz Imuta ("Poor Thing") embraces life on the West Coast with her ideal husband and two lovely daughters. When not laughing in her sleep or playing piano, she not-so-feverishly works on her novel. An aficionado of kombucha tea and dark chocolate, she understands the value of a slow simmer, the magic of life.

Jolie Kanat ("A Ferry Tale") of Marin County, California, is a professional writer in every medium. She has published a nonfiction book, *Bittersweet Baby*, columns for the *San Francisco Chronicle*, essays for *NPR Perspectives*, songs for Time Warner and Universal Studios, two CDs for children with special needs, and greetings cards for Schurmann Fine Papers.

Donna Karis ("On Patrol") lives in River Falls, Wisconsin, with her husband and three sons. Besides providing community education for a nonprofit agency, she is also writing a memoir about her middle son and how her family has coped with his epilepsy and special needs. She has contributed numerous articles to regional newspapers and magazines. To learn more about epilepsy: *www.cureepilepsy.org.*

Sandy Keefe ("Are You Done Feeling Sorry for Yourself?") is a registered nurse and the health-care manager at Camp Costanoan, a year-round camp for children and adults with disabilities in Cupertino, California. She is the proud mother of three children; Allie is now seventeen years old and a special needs cheerleader who continues to cope well with her medical challenges.

Chynna Tamara Laird ("The Greatest Gift") is a psychology student and freelance writer living in Edmonton, Alberta, Canada, with her three daughters—Jaimie, Jordhan, and baby Sophie—and her toddler son, Xander. Her work has appeared in many parenting, inspirational, Christian, and writing publications around the world. She's most proud of her recently published children's picture book, *I'm Not Weird, I Have SID.*

Patricia Ljutic ("Party Plans"), a writer, registered nurse, and mother of a bipolar child, writes often about her son's journey. Her work has appeared in the *Contra Costa Times*, *Marin Writes*, and *Circle Magazine*. She lives in Pinole, California.

Rachel McClain ("Speaking Up") is a freelance writer and mom living in Los Angeles. She has been published as a prize-winning author in *Women on Writing.* She has also been published in *Fuselit*, *Tuesday Shorts*, *Mom Writer's Literary Magazine*,

A Cup of Comfort® for Breast Cancer Survivors, and *A Cup of Comfort® for Military Families*.

Faith Paulsen ("Jacob's Treasure Map") lives in Norristown, Pennsylvania, with her family. Her work has appeared in *Literary Mama, Wild River Review, Open Salon*, and *Glimmer Train*. Her book, *Fun with the Family in Pennsylvania,* was published by Globe Pequot Press.

Lisa Peters ("A Life Less Perfect" and "Oh, the Perilous Paddleboats"), a writer, lives in Georgetown, Massachusetts, with her loving husband Jeffery and her two beautiful children, Weston and Nicholas. By sharing her family's experiences, she hopes to raise awareness of Prader-Willi syndrome, a rare and complex genetic disorder affecting the fifteenth chromosome. It causes low muscle tone, short stature, cognitive disabilities, incomplete sexual development, problem behaviors, and a chronic feeling of hunger that can lead to excessive eating and life-threatening obesity for the individual. For more information: *www.pwsausa.org*.

Mary C. M. Phillips ("He's Fine") has toured as a musician with various rock groups and musical comedy artists. She now composes contemporary Christian music and loves to write short stories. She resides in Long Island with her husband and son.

Vivian Joy Phillips ("Greater Than the Achievement") spent the majority of her life building a successful career in marketing and conference/event planning, while raising her children. She currently resides with her teenage boys and husband of four years in Quincy, Illinois, where she enjoys reading, spending time with family, volunteering, and working on her memoir.

Mona Rigdon ("Super–Model Mom") and her husband Keith live in Texarkana, Texas, with their four children, Tristan, Alyssa, Jasmine, and Gabby. A freelance writer of articles and essays, she works a "day job" as a paralegal in a general practice law firm. She also enjoys art, photography, and volunteering with her church, Boy Scouts, and Girl Scouts.

Debbie Roppolo ("Then a Hero Comes Along") is a freelance writer who resides in the Texas Hill Country with her husband and two sons. Between burning cookies and chasing after dogs wearing her nightclothes, she's written stories for national and regional magazines and newspapers. Her essays have appeared in several anthologies. For information on speech and/or learning delays: *www.education.com/topic/children-learning-disabilities/.*

Laura Shumaker ("A Regular Guy" and "A Tale of Two Brothers") is an award-winning writer and the author of *A Regular Guy: Growing Up with Autism*. A regular contributor to *NPR Perspectives*, her essays have appeared in *Voices of Autism* (LaChance, 2008), the *San Francisco Chronicle*, the *Contra Costa Times*, and *The Autism Advocate*.

Kathryn Lynard Soper ("Lighting the Way") is the mother of seven children, teenage to toddler. She is the author of *The Year My Son and I Were Born: A Story of Down Syndrome, Motherhood, and Self-Discovery* (Globe Pequot Press, 2009) and the editor of *Gifts: Mothers Reflect on How Children with Down Syndrome Enrich Their Lives* (Woodbine House, 2007).

B. J. Taylor ("Different on the Outside") is an award-winning freelance writer whose work has appeared in numerous anthologies, magazines, and newspapers. She has a wonderful husband, four children, and two adorable grandsons and makes her home in Huntington Beach, California.

Ellen Tomaszewski ("Reform School") and her husband Tom live in the state of Washington, where she writes full-time. Her recent memoir, *My Blindy Girl*, describes the struggles and growth of a mother learning to live with her child's visual disability. For information about achromatopsia: *www.achromatopsia.org.*

Ellen Ward ("Expletives Deleted"), on the heels of a successful career in advertising and freelance writing, turned fifty, prompting a midlife crisis and the launch of her independent full-service bookstore, FoxTale Book Shoppe, in Woodstock, Georgia. At FoxTale—where both writing and sign language classes are taught—Ellen indulges her passion for books and authors.

Wendy Hill Williams ("Riding a Bike") lives with her husband and two children in Northridge, California. She is a licensed marriage and family therapist and a part-time faculty member at California State University, Northridge, where she also teaches classes in the family studies department. Wendy is currently earning her PhD in health psychology and behavioral medicine.

Debbi Wise ("We're In This Together") was raised in Memphis, Tennessee, and lived for ten years in New Orleans, Louisiana. She wrote several one-act plays that were performed in the New Orleans area. Her story "Holiday Blockbuster" is featured in *The Ultimate Christmas* by Jeanne Bice (HCI, 2008). She now lives in Castle Rock, Colorado, with her husband, daughter, and a long-haired Dachshund named Scooter.

Deb Wuethrich ("The Gorilla Wore Roller Skates") is an Adrian, Michigan, resident and a staff writer for the weekly *Tecumseh Herald*. Deb was a 2003 recipient of an Amy Award of Outstanding Merit and has published in *Evangel*, *Woman's Touch*, and *Brave Hearts*. She and her husband Gordy have a spoiled rotten one-eyed cat named Lucy.

Mercedes M. Yardley ("Peanut Butter Toast") currently lives in Las Vegas. She somehow manages to write while staying at home with her children. She has been published in several online and print venues, and lives a life of happiness and red lipstick.

Sarah Yates ("A Vertical Victory") is a writer, mentor, and marketer. In Winnipeg, Canada, she formed Gemma B. Publishing to create literary heroes for the disabled. *Can't You Be Still?*, *Nobody Knows!*, and *Here's What I Mean to Say* each feature a heroine like her daughter, Gemma: feisty and independent.

About the Editor

Colleen Sell is the anthologist of more than thirty volumes of the *Cup of Comfort*® book series. She has also authored, ghostwritten, or edited numerous other books; published scores of articles; and served as editor-in-chief of two award-winning magazines. She and her husband, T. N. Trudeau, share an historic turn-of-the-century farmhouse, which they are perpetually renovating, on forty acres, which they are slowly turning into an organic blueberry, holly, and lavender farm, in the Pacific Northwest.